Hiking the Camino

CAMINO FRANCÉS

W
S ← → N
E

- Santiago de Compostela
- Arca
- Arzúa
- Melide
- Palas de Rei
- Portomarín
- Ferreiros
- Sarria
- Triacastela
- Cebreiro
- Vega de Valcarce
- Villafranca del Bierzo
- Ponferrada
- Rabanal
- Astorga
- Orbigo
- León
- Mansilla de las Mulas
- El Burgo Ranero
- Sahagún
- Cervatos
- Carrión de los Condes
- Frómista
- Castrojeriz
- Arroyo Sambol
- Burgos
- S. Juan de Ortega
- Belorado
- Santo Domino de la Calzada
- Nájera
- Longroño
- Los Arcos
- Estrella
- Puente la Reina
- Pamplona
- Monreal
- Roncesvalles
- Sangüesa
- St-Jean-Pied-de-Port
- Artieda
- Jaca
- Canfranc
- Somport
- Borce

HIKING THE CAMINO

500 Miles With Jesus

Father Dave Pivonka, T.O.R.

PUBLISHED BY ST. ANTHONY MESSENGER PRESS
CINCINNATI, OHIO

Cover and book design by Mark Sullivan
Cover photo provided by the author

LIBRARY OF CONGRESS CATALOGING-IN-PUBLICATION DATA
Pivonka, Dave.
Hiking the Camino : 500 miles with Jesus / Dave Pivonka.
p. cm.
Includes bibliographical references.
ISBN 978-0-86716-882-2 (pbk. : alk. paper) 1. Christian pilgrims and pilgrim-ages—Spain—Santiago de Compostela. 2. Pivonka, Dave—Travel—Spain—Santiago de Compostela. 3. Santiago de Compostela (Spain) —Description and travel. I. Title.
BX2321.S3P58 2009
263'.0424611—dc22
2009008926

ISBN 978-0-86716-882-2

Published by Servant Books, an imprint of St. Anthony Messenger Press
28 W. Liberty St.
Cincinnati, OH 45202
www.ServantBooks.org

Printed in the United States of America.

Printed on acid-free paper.

12 13 5 4 3

CONTENTS

ACKNOWLEDGMENTS

I walked the *Camino de Santiago* in order to say thank you to God for allowing me to be a priest for ten years. I love being a priest. I continue to be in awe at the fact that God called me and allows me to serve him and the Church as a priest. When I reflect on this, my heart cries out with gratitude.

I also want to thank God for Father Joe Lehman, T.O.R., who accompanied me every step of the way on my pilgrimage across Spain. Joe has been my friend and Franciscan brother for nearly twenty years, and I thank God for the gift he has been in my life. I truly doubt my Camino would have been possible had it not been for his companionship. Thanks for walking with me, Joe. I look forward to seeing what paths God leads us on in the future.

I suspect that for my twentieth anniversary as a priest, rather than walking across a foreign country, I will simply send God a thank-you card. This way he will have something to place on his refrigerator, and I will save myself a great deal of pain and agony. And so I dedicate this book as a humble offering of thanksgiving to God the Father for allowing me to be a priest forever of his Son, Jesus Christ.

INTRODUCTION

> pil-grim-age (noun) [pilgrimij]
> 1. a journey, esp. a long one, made to some sacred place
> as an act of religious devotion.
>
> . . . .
>
> Pil-grim (noun) [pilgrim]
> 1. any of the English Puritans who founded Plymouth
> Colony in Massachusetts in 1620.
> 2. one who goes on a long journey to a holy place for
> religious purposes.

We don't use the words *pilgrim* and *pilgrimage* much anymore. Sure, some people are vaguely familiar with the idea, but most Christians have never participated in a pilgrimage. This is a shame because the reality is that we are all pilgrims, and pilgrimages are tremendous opportunities for grace and conversion. I believe that pilgrimage is at the heart of the spiritual life.

Pope John Paul II put it well when preaching a homily in Australia in November 1986: "We are pilgrims progressing from time to eternity, and our goal is the Father himself. He constantly calls us beyond what is familiar and comfortable to new paths of faith and trust."[1]

Again, in November of 1988, the Holy Father wrote a message to the young people preparing for World Youth Day, which was to be held in Santiago, Spain, the following year:

Pilgrimage has a very deep spiritual significance; it can represent in itself an important form of catechesis.... In the world today there is a revival of the practice of going on pilgrimage, especially among the youth. Today, you are among those more inclined to experience a pilgrimage as a "way" to interior renewal, to a deepening of faith, a strengthening of the sense of communion and solidarity with your brothers and sisters and as a help in discovering your personal vocation. I feel sure that, thanks to your youthful enthusiasm, this year will see a new and rich development of the "Santiago Trail."[2]

This is the story of my pilgrimage on the "Santiago Trail" or the *Camino de Santiago de Compostela.* For thirty-one days I was a pilgrim walking across Spain, my destination being the burial place of Saint James. Along the path I discovered insights into the spiritual life that will forever change me. I was also reminded of other spiritual truths and was able to see and understand them with greater clarity. One learns a great deal about oneself, others and God when one walks day after day after day after day after day...

I invite you to join me on this journey. Open your heart and mind that the Holy Spirit may walk with you as you "walk" with me. I pray that my experiences and insights may draw you more deeply into the mystery and love of God.

Buen Camino (Good Journey)!

NOTES
1. John Paul II, homily in Canberra, Australia, November 24, 1986, no. 5, available at: www.vatican.va.
2. John Paul II, Message to the Youth of the World on the Occasion of the Fourth World Youth Day, November 27, 1988, no. 3, available at: www.vatican.va.

1: THE PLAN

I had been a Franciscan priest for eight years when I began thinking about what I wanted to do for my tenth anniversary. Many of my brother priests had taken an extended retreat, oftentimes for an entire month, and I knew that if this was something I was going to do, I would have to plan well in advance.

First I had to figure out what exactly I would do. All I knew for sure was that it needed to be a thanksgiving to God for allowing me to be a priest. I love being a priest!

I don't remember when I first heard about the Camino de Santiago. I must have been a kid, because it seems as if I have always been aware of it. I can only guess that I heard about it in school or saw it on TV, as I didn't know anyone who had taken this pilgrimage. Given the little I read as a kid, that was probably not my source, unless of course one of the Notre Dame football players spoke of it in an interview with *Sports Illustrated*.

One afternoon I was talking with a college student, and she mentioned that she was going to walk a part of the Camino de Santiago, "not the whole thing—that would take an entire month—but a part of it." Hmmm, an entire month?

I began to research the Camino. The more I read, the more excited I became. I started praying about the possibility of walking across Spain on the ancient pilgrimage route. Soon I knew in

1

my heart that this was the perfect way to thank God for allowing me to be a priest. I discussed this with my Franciscan religious superiors, and to my great delight all were very supportive.

I then called Father Joe, my classmate and one of my best friends, who would also be celebrating his tenth anniversary. I asked if he had any plans to mark this milestone. Given that it was still two years away, he stated that he thought his schedule was pretty free. I suggested that we take a walk, a long walk.

Father Joe had never heard of the Camino, but he was always up for an adventure. He said that he would pray about it and get back to me. In a few weeks he called and stated that he felt it would be a great opportunity. We decided that we would begin our pilgrimage in the late spring of 2006.

I didn't know at the time how physically challenging and spiritually enriching this experience would be. One of my fellow friars, who actually knew a great deal about the Camino, stated that he believed I would forever look at my life as "before and after the Camino." I thought that his evaluation was highly exaggerated but agreed that it would be a great experience.

I was wrong, and the friar was right. My life will never be the same, and I will forever look at it as "before and after the Camino."

The Camino

Santiago, a town in the westernmost part of Spain, is the traditional burial place of Saint James. The tradition is that upon the death of Jesus, Saint James sailed to Padrón, Galicia, and began preaching the gospel. Saint James stayed briefly in this region of Spain and eventually returned to Jerusalem, where he was that city's first bishop. In AD 42 Herod beheaded Saint James. His disciples brought his body back to Padrón, and he was buried in the village of Libredon, which would become Santiago.

Over the next many centuries, Santiago would remain a quiet little town, largely forgotten. However, in 813 a shepherd named Pelayo was startled by a group of bright lights hovering over a meadow where his flock was pastured. The "field" (*campo*) of "stars" (*estrellas*) gave us the traditional full name of the city, Santiago de Compostela. The local bishop declared that the shepherd had found the lost tomb of Saint James. The humble town of Santiago would never be the same.

This was a tumultuous time in Spain's history, with constant fighting between the Spanish Christians and the Moors. The Spanish people would continually pray to Saint James, and they attributed major victories to his intercession. Hence the fame of Saint James grew.

Records from as early as AD 950 speak of Christians making pilgrimages to Santiago de Compostela. In the Middle Ages it was one of three major pilgrimage destinations, Rome and Jerusalem being the other two. Because Santiago was rather accessible, and due to the many miracles that were attributed to Saint James, Santiago outshadowed all other pilgrimage sites. Tens of thousands of pilgrims journeyed there every year, from all parts of Europe, to pray at the tomb of the beloved disciple and visit the magnificent church dedicated to him.

It cannot be overestimated how significant these pilgrimage routes were to the development of Europe. Entire villages were formed for the sole purpose of taking care of pilgrims on their way to Santiago.

The late Middle Ages saw a decrease in pilgrimages, and in recent centuries pilgrimages have actually been quite rare.

However, UNESCO declared the Camino de Santiago a World Heritage Site in 1993, and the number of people walking the Camino is growing every year. In 1994 less than 15,000 people participated in the Camino, while 2004 (a Holy Year) saw over 170,000 pilgrims on the Camino. The average number of pilgrims over the last five years has been about 70,000 per year, with the majority of people walking in July, August and September.

People from literally all over the world walk the Camino for numerous reasons, most of them not religious. Many are simply looking for an adventure or want to be a part of history. The actress Shirley MacLaine walked the Camino many years ago and wrote about her experience. Apparently she discovered the meaning of the cosmos, including secrets of ancient civilizations, insights into human genesis and the essence of gender and sexuality. I am going to guess our experiences were quite different.

I was walking in order to thank God for letting me be a priest. Have I mentioned that I love being a priest?

Preparing for My Camino

I thoroughly enjoyed preparing for my Camino. I read a couple books on the topic and spent hours reading articles on the Internet. I also had numerous conversations with friends who had walked the Camino. With each conversation and each reading I became more excited. In many ways I had no idea what I was getting into, but I couldn't wait to get into it.

As the time was getting closer, I needed to make certain that I had the necessary supplies. As you can imagine, there are varying opinions of what an individual should and should not take, but the one thing everyone agreed upon was that good shoes and excellent socks are absolute necessities. On the Camino you live and die according to how your feet feel. The common opinion was that one may skimp on some things, but shoes and socks are not among them.

After a lot of reading and searching, I found a pair of hiking shoes that I thought would work, and I found three pairs of socks to make the trek with me. Little did I know that these socks would become my best friends and eventually the object of a minor miracle—not a major one but a minor one. Here is a list of the rest of the things that I brought:

Backpack
Sleeping bag (one-season)
Groundsheet
Inflatable neck pillow
Rain gear
Flashlight

Toiletries:
    Deodorant
    Quick-drying sports towel
    Toothbrush and paste
    Foot powder
    Lip balm
    Small comb
    Soap
    Toilet paper

First Aid Kit:
    Imodium
    Ibuprofen

Moleskin
2nd Skin Blister Pads
Sunscreen
Swiss Army Knife
String
Super-cool AAA-plus safety pins
Needle and thread

Clothes:
Bandannas, two
Hat
Rain jacket
Lightweight sweatshirt
Long pants that could be made into shorts
Shorts
Quick-drying shirts, three
Underwear, three pairs
Sandals

Miscellaneous:
Camera
1.5 liter water bottles, two
Watch (with alarm)
Sunglasses
Passport
Supply of plastic bags (wet weather "handbags")
Playing cards
Earplugs
Guide book

Spiritual:
Divine Office
Bible
Mass kit (because I'm a priest)
Journal and pen
Rosary

Most of the articles I read stated that you should aim to have your backpack at about 10 percent of your body weight. That would mean mine would weigh about eighteen pounds or eight kilos. (Almost all of the materials I was reading used the metric system —you know, the one we had to learn in second grade and soon forgot.) I am pretty low maintenance and am used to traveling light, so I did not think this was going to be a problem at all.

However, the one thing that none of the articles took into account was the various items I would need given that I am a priest. Father Joe and I were going to celebrate Mass every day as well as pray together, and this would mean we would need everything for Mass, our prayer books and the Scriptures. Slowly but surely I crept my way up to my eighteen-pound limit and beyond.

As the day for departure came closer and closer, I loaded and unloaded my pack dozens of times. I did my best to weigh my pack (I didn't have a very accurate scale) and quickly came to realize that there was no way I was going to be able to get it down to eighteen pounds. I got rid of absolutely everything that was not essential and decided that I would still be carrying extra weight. I didn't know exactly what the pack weighed, but it didn't matter, as there was nothing I could leave behind.

I was actually quite impressed at how little I was taking, and as I slipped on my pack it truly felt great. Of course I only had the pack on for about a minute, and once on the road I would learn that twenty pounds could just as well be two hundred.

Getting in Shape

There are many routes to Santiago; the route we chose is one of the most traditional, called the *Camino Francés*. It begins in Saint-Jean-Pied-de-Port, France; from there it crosses the Pyrenees and enters north central Spain, then continues west to Santiago.

The first and last third of the route are hilly and mountainous, while the middle third is flat farmland. This particular route is five hundred miles or eight hundred kilometers, which I think sounds longer.

For the month before the Camino, I walked about four or five times a week. Given that I was living in Gaming, Austria, at the time, I would hike the hills in the area, which I enjoyed greatly. I also participated in other sporting activities, so I felt that I was in good shape.

At this point I was mostly concerned about breaking in my shoes and getting used to the backpack. Everything felt fantastic; this was going to be great! Oh, how naïve I was.

While there were a million practical things to do to prepare for my pilgrimage, more important was my spiritual preparation. I would have to say that I fell a little short in this, but my time preparing for the pilgrimage was very blessed.

I spent quite a bit of time reading about the various saints who are associated with the Camino. (Saint Francis, for example, walked the Camino and started several friaries along the route to Santiago.) I began to ask these saints to pray for me, that my heart would be open to all God had planned for me. I wanted to be able to surrender my plan and my agenda and let God have free reign.

Most of my time preparing spiritually was in eucharistic adoration in the Sacred Heart Chapel, which is a small side chapel of a glorious Gothic church in Gaming. The chapel was built in 1342, and it is a wonderfully holy little place where Carthusian monks prayed for nearly five hundred years. It is now home for the study-abroad program of Franciscan University, of which I was the director.

My spiritual preparation was really very simple. I prayed that I would be able to offer God my Camino as a humble offering of thanksgiving for allowing me to be a priest. I also prayed that Jesus would use the Camino to make me holy. "It's all I've ever truly wanted, Jesus: just to be holy."

The weeks before I began the hike, I prayed for a word or phrase that I could hold on to for the Camino. As I prayed I continued to be struck by the words "All this for the King." So this became the theme for my Camino. I was going to do "all this for the King." It should be noted that I had no idea what *this* meant.

Time to Go

The days before we left for France, I asked myself a number of times whether I had done all I needed to do. I checked and rechecked lists to make sure I had not forgotten anything. The bottom line was that I wanted to make sure I was prepared as well as possible.

But when it came right down to it, I really did not know what I was getting into. I didn't know what it would be like to get up every day for thirty-one days and walk. I wasn't sure how meals were going to work. I didn't really understand how we would find where we were going. I was not sure if I had everything I needed, and I wondered if I had forgotten something.

However, I knew there was going to be a day when I would finally have to begin. I had to trust that I had prepared as I should and that everything would work out. I needed to take that first step. It wasn't until I had actually started that I would know for sure if my pack was too heavy or if I was going to get blisters from my shoes. I had to believe I was prepared, and I had to start. It was that simple.

There are moments in life when we simply have to start walking. We often don't know exactly where we are going or how we are going to get there, but we know that if we are going to move on, if we are going to arrive at our destination, we must begin to walk.

And so I was ready to begin, having little idea what lay ahead but trusting that God would lead me.

2 : 'TWAS THE NIGHT
BEFORE THE CAMINO

I was filled with excitement and anticipation. I could hardly believe that Father Joe and I were going to finally begin the Camino. I had prayed, planned and looked forward to this for about two years, and the time for departure had finally come.

Father Joe and I flew from Vienna, Austria, to Biarritz, France. From there it was a thirty-minute taxi ride to Saint-Jean-Pied-de-Port, which was our starting place for the Camino.

Saint-Jean-Pied-de-Port, in southeastern France, is a lovely medieval town. I walked down the narrow cobblestone streets lined with charming houses made of rock and surrounded by red, purple and yellow flowers. The town had a feel of antiquity, and I felt as if I had been beamed there by some time machine.

Everything was perfect: It was a beautiful day, with the sun shining and a few feathery clouds aimlessly drifting nowhere. Dozens of pilgrims meandered through the slender streets. Many had their backpacks and walking staffs and seemed to be as excited as I was. Most people had a shell attached to their packs, which is a traditional sign for the pilgrim on the Camino. I couldn't wait to get my shell and walking staff. Then I would really be a pilgrim.

The air was thick with anticipation.

Pointing the Way

The first stop in Saint-Jean-Pied-de-Port was the pilgrims' office, where we would obtain our credentials. It took Father Joe and me a while to find the office; we got kind of lost. How were we going to walk across Spain if we couldn't even find the office where the journey began?

The credentials are a type of passport for the Camino. Mine identified me as a pilgrim, and as such I was given certain benefits. One benefit was being able to stay in an *albergue*, which is the Spanish name for the hostels that house pilgrims. The albergues are very inexpensive, with some only asking for a donation, while most range from three to six euros a night.

I discovered that I would have to show my credentials at each albergue, where they would be stamped. Upon completion of the pilgrimage, I would need to present my credentials to the pilgrims' office in Santiago to confirm the fact that I had walked the Camino. At this point I would then receive my *Compostela*, a certificate stating that I had completed the Camino de Santiago.

The stamped credentials would also make for a wonderful souvenir, having dozens of distinct stamps from all across the Camino. One could liken it to a passport with stamps from various countries. The more I learned, the more excited I became about beginning the Camino the following morning.

We took care of a few other details at the pilgrims' office. We were given a very brief introduction to the Camino. First on my mind was how we were supposed to know where to go. One of the gentlemen taking care of us confidently stated, "This is easy; just follow the *flechas amarillas* [yellow arrows]. Don't worry: You can't miss them, and you won't get lost."

Lord knows, I had heard that before. Please, were simple

flechas amarillas really going to guide us all the way across Spain?

While I was daydreaming about *flechas amarillas*, I noticed other pilgrims going through their backpacks and sorting their things. I didn't understand what they were doing. A gentleman then asked if I wanted to weigh my backpack. He stated that lots of times people bring too much stuff and have to get rid of some of it. Aha, I understood why the other pilgrims were going through their things.

I was pretty sure that I did not have a bunch of excess luggage but was curious to see exactly what my pack weighed. I placed it on a type of meat hook, and it came in at about twenty-six pounds. I was hoping that it would be closer to eighteen, but I really didn't have anything that I could get rid of, so I determined that I would simply have to carry a few more pounds. The man in the office stated that it was not bad but did suggest that I try to get rid of a little weight. "Every kilo counts when you are walking six to eight hours a day."

Finally I was given my shell, my *concha*. Most statues of Saint James have him with a walking staff, a wide-brimmed hat and a concha. The concha has been a distinguishing symbol of the pilgrim to Santiago for over a thousand years. I proudly received mine and proceeded to tie it to my backpack next to a small wooden Franciscan tau cross that I was also carrying.

I already had the hat, and now that I had my concha, I was beginning to look and feel like a pilgrim. I would get my walking staff later, and then my accessories would be complete.

A gentleman from the office escorted Father Joe and me to our first albergue, where we would stay the night. Our host for the evening was Janine, a lovely elderly French woman who did not speak a word of English. Given that I do not speak a word of French, she and I got along perfectly.

We were shown to our room, which was up a flight of rickety stairs and down a narrow hall. It was a very small, plain, square room with three sets of bunk beds. Our roommates for the evening were Mario from Italy and Jad from Hungary. There was a third guy who seemed very quiet and secretive. He never offered his name and kept his distance. I deduced that he was running from the law and wanted to keep a low profile.

Our final roommate was a young *woman* from Austria. This was certainly going to be an interesting month.

As it was about time for dinner, I went to a local market and grabbed some tomato sauce, pasta and a bottle of wine, which came to a grand total of five euros. Father Joe and I cooked dinner and enjoyed our last supper before the Camino. We then walked to the church Notre-Dame-du-Bout-du-Pont (Our Lady by the Bridge), to take some time to pray before we began walking the following morning. And there the Lord spoke to me.

The First Lesson

Sitting in the silence of a dark, musty, medieval church, I could feel the presence of God. I was flooded with all kinds of emotions. I was so excited to finally be beginning my Camino, but it was a nervous excitement. I felt as if I were beginning a journey but did not know what I would find. I was searching for something but was not sure what it was or how I would find it.

One of my students had told me that the Camino is Jesus, so my prayer was that I would find Jesus. He is the one for whom I am always searching, and I prayed with all my heart that it would be he that I would find. Ultimately, I believe that it is Jesus that every human heart seeks. It is only his peace, his joy, his comfort, his healing, his forgiveness and his love that will satisfy the longing of every human soul. I wanted to find him more deeply and allow him to find me.

I know that some prayers are scarier than others, and I offered a prayer that caused me a little bit of fear, all the while knowing that it was absolutely necessary that I began this way: "Jesus, I give you permission to do whatever needs to happen to me in order to bring me to conversion and greater holiness." Little did I know what was to happen over the next thirty-one days. God would hear and grant my prayer.

As I was sitting in the church trying to focus on spiritual things, I couldn't help but think about my pack. (I didn't know at the time that this would be a major focus of my thoughts over the coming days and weeks.) I was surprised that it weighed twenty-six pounds; I really thought that I had packed light. In my mind I started going through everything in the pack, wondering what I could do without.

After several minutes of this a light came on. "Lord, perhaps this is where we begin. Not with my pack but with my heart, my very life. What is it that you want me to get rid of? How do you want to strip me? How do you want to empty me? What excess luggage am I carrying in my soul?" I sat in stillness and prayed.

I firmly believe that at the heart of the spiritual life is detachment. The spiritual life is not about building up or acquiring; rather, it is about being stripped, being emptied. It is my desire to get rid of everything in my life that is not Christ so that he alone can be seen. As Saint Paul reminds me, it is not about me but Christ who lives in me (see Galatians 2:20).

Being emptied or stripped is difficult and often involves suffering, but I believe it is really the only way to be free. God emptied himself and became man (see Philippians 2:7-10), so I too need to see that I am emptied till only God remains.

In the stillness of this chapel, even before I had begun walking, I could sense the Lord telling me that in fact I was carrying things that he might be inviting me to leave behind. I prayed for the grace to say yes.

So in the peace and quiet of a simple baroque church dedicated to Our Lady, in a small town in southern France, I whispered a prayer to begin my Camino: "Lord, I will leave anything you ask. Please, just show me what. I will do all this for you, my King."

And so it began.

I returned to my albergue determined to leave something behind. After several minutes I came to grips with a few things that I did not *absolutely* need: a small hand towel and the groundsheet. I placed the items on a table in the albergue that had been provided for this very purpose. Apparently I was not the first to feel the need to leave a few things behind.

Satisfied, I went to bed at about nine o'clock, with dreams of what was to come walking through my head.

3 : IN THE BEGINNING

Father Joe and I began the Camino on Thursday, May 18. We wanted to be in Santiago on Saturday, June 17, the Vigil of Corpus Christi. We thought it would be great to finish the Camino on such a special feast day. If things went more slowly than anticipated, we could finish on Sunday, June 18, and still catch our plane Monday, June 19. We absolutely had to be in Santiago by then, or our walk was going to be much, much longer.

On the first day I woke up without an alarm at 5:45 AM. I think I may have been a little excited. I got all of my things together, which took longer than I had anticipated. I knew that over time I would become more efficient. I had a light breakfast of hot tea, bread and jam and was ready to go by 7:00.

I experienced a feeling of exhilaration as Father Joe and I began walking. I had been planning, reading, studying and praying for over two years for this pilgrimage, and I had finally begun. I was walking the *Camino de Santiago de Compostela*. As I exited Saint-Jean, I wondered what the next five hundred miles would hold for me.

But first things first, we had to figure out how exactly to exit Saint-Jean. The words of the gentleman in the pilgrims' office rang through my mind: "Just follow the yellow arrows." I felt like Dorothy in *The Wizard of Oz*.

We passed through the *Porte d'Espagne*, and I noticed a small wooden statue of the Madonna and Child pointing me on the right path. This was a good sign. Soon we crossed an ancient rock bridge and came to the first fork in the road. Hmm, which way do we go?

I was pleased to see a small blue sign with a yellow arrow pointing to Roncesvalles. It was just as the gentleman at the office had said! So far so good. The sign stated that the trek should take about six and a half hours, but I didn't have any idea how quickly we would walk.

In what I consider to be God's sense of humor, the first day takes the pilgrim over some of the most difficult terrain of the entire pilgrimage. The walk from Saint-Jean-Pied-de-Port to Roncesvalles, Spain, is fifteen and a half miles. This is not a terribly long walk, but what makes it difficult is that it is uphill. The elevation at the beginning was 550 feet, and by the time we would arrive at our albergue for the night, we would have climbed through the Pyrenees to over 4,750 feet. Talk about a baptism by fire.

It was a cool morning and very cloudy; it looked as if it could rain at any minute. However, there was no way my spirits were going to be rained on. I was walking, and that was the only thing that mattered.

As the day went on it became foggier and foggier. The higher we climbed, the more unpleasant the weather became. By midday we were actually walking in the clouds. While it never actually rained, it drizzled and was just wet.

At around eleven o'clock we took a break to eat the lunch that we had packed. It was some bread, sausage, cheese and fruit, and it tasted wonderful. I really felt good and was surprised that I was not in the least bit tired. All the talk about how difficult the Camino is was grossly exaggerated, I concluded.

Check In

We arrived at Roncesvalles at around 2:00, which meant the walk took us seven hours. Considering the fact that the sign at the beginning said it should take six and a half and adding in the lunch break, I felt pretty good.

Once we arrived we began what would be a similar routine for the next month. First we checked into the albergue. I presented my pilgrim passport to the attendant and received my first stamp. Perhaps it was childish, but I was thrilled. My first stamp!

This particular albergue was a large Gothic building built entirely of stone. It had only one main sleeping room, containing over a hundred bunk beds made of cold gray metal and grouped in sets of two, so four people shared a set of bunks. I was pretty sure this was not going to be my best night's sleep.

Father Joe and I were not the first people to arrive, so clothing, shoes and bedding were scattered all over the room, not unlike my room as a teenager. I felt right at home. We picked the first two open beds and threw our sleeping bags on them. This would be our home for the night.

I looked around to see who my neighbors were going to be. To the left were a couple of guys who appeared to be from Brazil, and to the right a couple of gals who I think were from Germany. I have to admit I was a little surprised that there was no separation between men and women and even more bewildered by the freedom that many felt in changing their clothes in the middle of the room. Clearly I was not in Kansas anymore.

It's not as if there was no bathroom in which people could change. It was located down a flight of stairs. I was amazed by how small the facilities were but was pleased that the men's and women's facilities were separate. There were only two showers for about seventy-five men, and the thought of a warm shower to end the day quickly retreated.

Upon getting settled into the albergue, it was time to wash my clothes. On the side of the building were multiple faucets with washbasins. The water was freezing, so washing did not take long. Since there was no clothesline, I hung my wet clothes from the metal bars on my bed. Then we set out for dinner.

This particular albergue did not have kitchen facilities, so Father Joe and I had dinner at a local place that was advertising "Pilgrims' Meals." There were two sittings, and we took the early one at 5:30. It was a wonderful dinner of soup, fresh trout, potatoes, dessert and wine, all for eight euros each, which I thought was a very good deal.

Two couples from Germany and a couple from Wisconsin joined Father Joe and me. Everyone was rather animated from that first day on the Camino, and we all enjoyed sharing stories of how we got to Roncesvalles. It was a fantastic time together.

Evening Quiet

Finally the majority of pilgrims gathered in the church for the Pilgrims' Mass. Father Joe and I concelebrated, and it was a very moving liturgy.

For the most part the Mass was in Spanish, but throughout the liturgy other languages were used, making for a brilliant experience of the universality of the Catholic Church. It was evident that many of the people at Mass were not Catholic, but everyone seemed to be moved by the liturgy and participated as they were able.

The end was particularly touching. Right before the final blessing, several priests entered the sanctuary. They were there to offer the Pilgrims' Blessing, which would be given in about a dozen different languages.

Priest: O God, be a companion for them along the path, a guide at crossroads, strength in their weariness, defense before dangers, shelter on the way, shade against heat, light in the darkness, a comforter in their discouragements and firmness in their intentions, in order that, through your guidance, they might arrive unscathed at the end of their journey, and enriched with graces and virtues, they might return safely to their homes, which will not lament their absence, filled with salutary and lasting joy.

All: Amen.

Priest: May the Lord direct your steps with his approval and be your inseparable companion on the entire Camino.

All: Amen.

Priest: May the Virgin Mary grant you maternal protection, defend you in all dangers of soul and body, and may you merit to arrive safely at the end of your pilgrimage under her mantle.

All: Amen.

Priest: May the archangel Raphael accompany you on the Camino as he accompanied Tobias and protect you from every injury and obstacle.

All: Amen.

The simple ritual was beautiful and exceedingly moving. I had a sense of being a part of something that was much bigger than myself. I could imagine the millions of pilgrims over the centuries who had walked on the very stones and paths on which I was walking. I could visualize each pilgrim carrying his or her own petitions, cares, worries, hopes and dreams on this journey of faith.

What an amazingly fantastic day it had been, what a blessed beginning. As I lay in bed, I was surprised at how good I felt. Some of the other pilgrims were talking about how sore they were, but my body felt really great. I was pretty sure that all the talk about how hard the Camino was and how much it hurt your body was exaggerated. Clearly I had trained well. I could honestly say that my body did not hurt at all.

I was tired and desired sleep, but I was also exhilarated at what had taken place and what was happening. I thanked God for the amazing day and for how blessed I was to be on pilgrimage. "God, you are so good to me. Thank you." I spent time praying and wondering what God wanted to show me and teach me on the Camino. I was overwhelmed with a tremendous sense of his blessing.

It was eerie: I was in bed surrounded by over two hundred people whom I had never met, and I felt at home. It seemed so right, so natural and so normal. It was peaceful.

I listened to the breathing of my fellow pilgrims. Among all these people in various states of sleep or restlessness, there was a strange calm and a type of peaceful dissonance. I drifted off to sleep knowing that God was present.

4 : REALITY CHECK

You duped me, O Lord, and I allowed myself to be duped! (see Jeremiah 20:7).

On second thought, maybe this was going to kill me. My body hurt badly: my shoulders, my feet, my back and a bunch of other muscles whose location and function I didn't know exactly. What had gone wrong?

The end of the second day really was quite miserable. I didn't know who had gotten to my pack over the night, but I am almost certain that it was a good fifteen to twenty pounds heavier than it had been the day before.

We began walking that second day at around 7:15, and I was finished by around noon. The only problem was that we still had another two hours and forty-five minutes before we arrived at Larrasoaña, which was our destination for the day.

Every step of the last several hours hurt. It was as if I was walking on needles. Where the day before had been wonderful and peaceful and somewhat euphoric, the latter part of this second day was wretched. I was surprised at how sore my feet were. We were only walking about fifteen miles, but the end was horrible.

As I trudged forward I prayed; I prayed a lot. In the midst of the discomfort I found myself repeating my theme for the Camino, "All this for the King, all this for the King." I soon realized that the pain in my body was the *this* in "All *this* for the

King." I knew God was inviting me to give everything about the Camino to Christ.

As I walked I told Christ, "It is not I who simply hurt, but I who hurt for you. I give *this* to you. I do *this* for you."

I will never be able to explain the presence of God I felt at that moment. The pain had meaning: It was not an end, but it led me someplace else, to someone. For that brief moment there was a communion between God and me that was ineffable.

Made It

We did eventually arrive at our destination. Larrasoaña is a small town with a beautiful little brook running through it. Most of the homes and buildings look tired and worn and are colorless due to the old rock construction. However, the town does have a beauty in its simplicity. Like most of the towns I would walk through, the church is in the middle, and everything surrounds the church plaza.

We checked in at our albergue, which was a two-floor facility with about twenty sets of bunks on each floor. It was a little nicer than the previous night's in that it was not so large. I crawled up to the second floor, dropped my bag next to my bed and flopped down. I just lay there, not wanting to move. Who am I trying to kid? I lay there not able to move.

After a while I began to feel a little better. I mustered enough energy to want to go take a shower and wash my clothes. Sometime after this I rallied enough oomph to actually go and take a shower and wash my clothes.

The shower room was a type of trailer outside the albergue. What was interesting was that the room doubled as a kind of phone booth. Apparently it was one of the few places where pilgrims could plug in their cell phones. The room was packed with people talking, and quickly I realized that it was not going to empty soon. I proceeded to take my cold shower with a dozen or so conversations, mostly in French, filling my thoughts. Life is different on the Camino.

Given that the albergue did not have kitchen facilities, we once again ate at a local place offering a pilgrims' meal, a wonderful white bean soup followed by pork chops and veggies and a magnificent red wine. It was fantastic.

At dinner with me this night were Father Joe, a woman from Denmark in her mid-fifties who was walking the Camino for the second time, a gentleman also in his mid-fifties from England and two young Italian women in their early twenties. English really is the international language, and we had a great time telling one another where we were from and why we were walking the Camino.

The woman from Denmark had recently recovered from cancer and wanted to walk the Camino once again as a sign of her "restoration." The Italian women were actually making a pilgrimage for religious purposes. "I need to get some things right in my life," said one. The gentleman was searching: for what he was not sure.

If I were to identify the most common reason for people to walk the Camino, I would say that is it: searching. People are not exactly sure what they are looking for, but they know that there is something lacking in their lives, and they hope to find what that is on the Camino.

My companions at dinner were very interesting, and their stories were engaging. It quickly became clear to me that dinnertime was going to be a lot of fun on the Camino.

The Real World

After dinner Father Joe and I celebrated Mass. Given that the church was locked, we prayed Mass next to the beautiful little stream that ran through the town.

Later in the evening I was praying and reflecting on the second day, and it occurred to me that my Camino actually was like the spiritual life. I remembered being in a small chapel, back when I first had become serious about following Christ, and, pouring out my heart to God, telling him that I wanted to live no longer for myself but for him. At that moment I had an experience of God and his Holy Spirit that would forever change me. In many ways this was the beginning of my adult walk with Christ.

The following days and weeks were amazing. Daily prayer times were moving, the Scriptures came alive, and the grace of the sacraments was palpable. Everything was wonderful.

But then something strange happened. The euphoric feeling didn't last. I recall going to prayer and actually not having much to say and not hearing God say anything to me. I was pretty sure I was experiencing the "dark night of the soul."

Over time I came to understand that what I was going through was actually quite normal: It was the spiritual life. Many people experience a real excitement and zeal at the beginning of their faith walk, but that walk eventually becomes difficult. I came to understand that it was at that point, the moment where the spiritual life became difficult, that my faith became more real.

"What now, Dave? What do you do now that you don't have all the warm feelings, all the consolation? Now that you are not totally sure what I am saying or what I am asking or where I am leading? What will you do now?"

Well, I began "walking" once more. Perhaps not with all the fanfare or excitement but certainly with better clarity of what the spiritual life really is and what may await me. Following Christ, the spiritual life, is not simply about those first exciting days. It is about days that are hard, days filled with trials, days that are dull and empty with seemingly nothing happening. But we keep on walking because this is a part of life, and it is the only way to get to a place of rest. I often need to be reminded that this is the spiritual *life*, not a day, week, month or year.

Before going to bed I spent a few more minutes praying and asking for strength. I really wanted to use every moment and every experience as an opportunity to grow closer to God. I wrote in my journal before I went to sleep for the night, "Dear Lord, I know that you will make my body stronger. May you also make my heart strong."

What a shame it would be if I finished the Camino with my legs and body in tremendous shape but my heart unchanged.

5 : THE WEIGHT OF THE CROSS

I met Pablo the first night of the Camino. He was a young guy, somewhere in his mid-twenties. He was in the bunk next to me, and it looked as if he was alone.

I noticed that he was wearing a cool soccer jersey from Brazil, and I asked him if he spoke English and if he was a fan. He said yes to both. (The World Cup would be starting in a couple of weeks in Germany, so it was a popular conversation topic.) He was from Brazil and absolutely loved Brazilian soccer. "It's more like poetry than soccer. It is beautiful."

I didn't grow up watching soccer, but my previous year in Europe had increased my respect for one of the few truly world sports. I had learned enough to know that Brazil was always one of the favorites in the World Cup.

Over the next few days I ran into Pablo several times, and we would say hi and briefly chat. He was quiet and reserved, but he seemed to enjoy speaking English with me. He would often wear his Brazil jersey, and while I liked it, it was his backpack that I absolutely loved.

Pablo's pack was amazingly small. I'm talking first backpack, kindergarten, Spiderman Collection small. I fear that I actually came to covet his backpack.

"O Lord, if only my backpack were as small as his, I know that I could carry it without complaining." What I could not understand was how Pablo could fit all his things in that little pack.

Compared to most of the other packs, mine was pretty much in the middle, not that big but not exactly small either. I like to think it was simple. Some packs were so stuffed and had a dozen different items hanging from them. The only things I had hanging from my pack were my concha, my Franciscan cross and my sleeping bag, which was attached to the bottom of the pack. Every now and then my socks were still damp in the morning, so I would hang them off the back as well.

My backpack really was a great one, but I was growing tired of carrying it. I was fairly convinced that it was more of a burden than *anyone* else's. But I suffered in relative silence.

Heavy Issues

The goal for the day was Pamplona. When I was planning my Camino, I actually toyed with arranging the timing so that I would reach Pamplona when the bulls were running. I would love to run with the bulls. I know, I know, it's silly, foolish, crazy and dangerous (I have heard it all from my mother), but for some reason I can't explain, I would love to do it.

I learned that the only requirements for running with the bulls are that one be male, sober and dressed in white. I was sure I could handle all three of those. Unfortunately, the bulls run in mid-July, and I wasn't able to walk at that time.

An enormous digital clock met me in Pamplona. It read *46-22-3-8,* and it was counting down by the second. It took me a minute to figure out that this was a countdown until the bulls ran: 46 days, 22 hours, 3 minutes and 8, 7, 6, 5 seconds.

"Why must I be taunted? One day I will run with the bulls!"

When Father Joe and I checked in at the albergue, I was right behind Pablo. It worked out that we would be in the same room. As soon as we were settled, Pablo ran off to take a shower. I noticed his pack sitting next to his bed. This was my chance, and I was going to take it!

I made sure Pablo was in the bathroom and ran back to our room. "Father Joe, it's driving me crazy. I have got to see how light that pack is."

So with Pablo in the shower, I slipped his pack onto my shoulder. I couldn't believe it. Rather than being light, it was like lead. How could that be? I wondered what on earth he could be carrying that would cause it to weigh so much. Gold coins?

Now I was really curious. I just had to find out what was in the pack. However, responding to grace, and the fact that I heard Pablo coming back from the shower, I virtuously resisted the desire to open his pack and look inside.

Mine Alone

Praying later that night, it did not take much time for me to figure out what God was trying to say to me. We each have our own cross (pack) to bear. What looks to be a light load may in fact be very heavy, and what appears to be heavy may be light. What is important is that we each have our cross to bear and that God knows what is ours to handle. There is no way we can look at someone else and be able to know the exact nature or weight of his or her cross. This is known only to God and to that person.

We all have crosses, and we all suffer. I recall someone saying to me one time that I couldn't understand what she was going through because I had never suffered. Of course, this is ridiculous, but I suppose someone could look at my life and say I have had it pretty easy. But how can you tell? I am not aware of any type of gauge that one is able to read to determine the weight of one's cross, the measure of one's suffering.

One of my greatest crosses would have to be sitting down with person after person, day after day, listening to their pain and struggles and not being able to take them all away. It is such a helpless feeling. I so want people to be freed of their burdens and am fully aware of my inability to do that. I can't explain how difficult it is to listen to people tell me of the abuse they suffered as children and not be able to fix their broken hearts. To see the hollow look in someone's face and the dark gaze of their eyes and know that in the end this is a road that this person must walk down and a cross he or she must carry.

Of course, I do my best to walk with people who are suffering and to love them, but in the end they have to carry their own crosses. Through prayer I try to bring them to a place where they know that God will be with them and they understand that he alone can heal them and help them bear their crosses. But this takes time. At the very moment I am talking with someone, the suffering is painful, and promises of the future glory are often too distant to see or believe in.

To be invited into someone else's suffering and to journey with him or her is both humbling and a cross. It has also been one of my greatest blessings, for it has been one of the ways God has broken me and brought me to conversion. God has used these experiences time and time again to lead me closer to his heart. At these very moments I come face-to-face with my limitedness and my helplessness and am invited to totally abandon myself to God. At these moments God beckons me and invites me to receive his strength. I turn to him because I have nowhere else to go, and this is ultimately a good place to be.

The cross for many a parent or grandparent, or anyone really, is watching a loved one suffer and knowing that, for reasons we can't fully understand, this is the loved one's cross, and we can only watch the person carry it. I can't count the number of times parents have come to me asking for prayer for their son or daughter, and their pain and suffering is literally etched in their faces.

I regularly wonder, what is a greater suffering: my own pain or helplessly watching those I love suffer? How difficult must it have been for Mary to be at the cross watching her son die, helpless to stop it, unable to free him from his pain. What suffering!

We each have our crosses to carry. I recall one Italian woman who was having a really hard time. She had over twenty-six blisters on her feet! For a while her fellow pilgrims helped her carry her backpack, but we all knew that she was going to have to eventually take it back. It was hers and hers alone, and no one could carry it for her.

However, we must remember that Jesus was the first to carry the cross, and he is able to give us the strength and grace to be able to carry ours. Some of the most profound experiences of Christ I had on the Camino, as well as in my life, have been while suffering. When I embrace my cross, I find Jesus.

Our God knows what it is to suffer. The one who accepted the weight of humanity's cross on his back so that my cross would not break me, he really does know; he does understand. My cross has been chosen out of love for me, and I continually pray for the grace to accept it in the love with which it was given. I pray that carrying my cross will lead me to Jesus and his deep love for me. Amazing isn't it? All of this from Pablo's little backpack.

6 : FOR LOVE'S SAKE

I first met Mara at breakfast. The albergue I was staying in offered breakfast, which I must say was a stretch to call "breakfast" by American standards. It consisted of stale bread, jam and hot tea. But it was free, and it was ready when I got up in the morning, so I took advantage of it.

I sat down next to Mara, and we exchanged some small talk. After a few minutes I was finished and said good-bye. I had a feeling we would run into each other again.

And we did, about an hour into the day's walk, at one of the most truly unique stops on the Camino. It was the Irache Monastery with its *Fuente del Vino*. The Irache Monastery was built in the tenth century to serve the needs of the pilgrims. It no longer serves as a monastery, but it definitely still serves the pilgrims. It boasts one of the most famous fountains on the entire Camino, because unlike the thousand-some other fountains, this one gives the weary pilgrim a choice: water or wine.

Two spigots protruding from an ancient stone wall welcome visiting pilgrims. The fountain on the right states *agua*, while the other, with a red-stained basin, offers *vino*.

This was one of the few times I waited in line to fill my "water" bottle. What a sight! Pilgrim after pilgrim poured water from their bottles in order to fill them with the obvious beverage of choice. I would have to say that it was not the best wine I have ever had, but it was probably the most successful "water" stop. Either by the grace of God or the fruit of the vine, the next several hours of walking were pain free.

I met Mara as she was topping off her tank. We chatted for a few minutes, and she began walking with Father Joe and me. She would be our welcome companion for the next three days. It was nice having another person with which to share the walk, and Father Joe and I enjoyed Mara's company.

The first day we chatted about simple things like where we were from, family background and favorite music and movies. Most of the movies and music groups Mara mentioned I had never seen or heard of. It would be fair to say that she and I had very different tastes and saw the world quite differently.

As I prayed that evening, I found myself praying for Mara. I wrote in my journal that she had a dear heart but that I thought she had been hurt a lot. I also wrote that she and I probably disagreed on almost every theological point, but that God had brought us together and he wanted me to learn from the encounter. When I was praying for her, I asked God what he wanted me to say to her, and I felt him say, "For now, just love her."

"OK. I hope I can do this well."

Finally there was the issue of her name. I don't know why, but it just didn't feel right. I wrote her name as "Mara," with quotes, not really knowing why. I just felt that there was something not right about "Mara."

Walk and Learn

The next morning "the three *amigos*," as a fellow pilgrim referred to Father Joe, Mara and me, left at about 6:45. As was usually the case, my body felt pretty good in the morning. The beginning of the walk was through a lovely park with beautiful soft green grass. The morning was spectacular. There was a light dew, which allowed us to see our footprints, like footprints on sand.

While the sun was just peeking over the horizon, our three bodies cast giant shadows on the field in front of us. We had a great time acting out various goofy postures and laughing at the shadows we created. It was an amusing morning.

Since I was wondering, sometime later in the morning I asked Mara what her name meant. "Is it a derivative of *Mary*?" I asked.

I don't know what exactly happened—there was some kind of interruption—but Mara never answered the question. So later in the day I asked her again. She paused and then told me that Mara was not her real name. She had decided before the Camino to take the name of Mara while on the pilgrimage. She explained that the name means "bitterness or sorrow" and that it was her hope to leave those behind on the Camino. I would later learn that the name was taken from George MacDonald's book *Lilith*.

I remember being struck at how beautiful and humble Mara's insight was. I could imagine her leaving wounded parts behind her with each step she took. I found myself praying a lot for her and continually feeling God ask me to simply walk with her. It was not about my convincing her of something but just being with her, caring for her and enjoying her company.

One of the things Mara taught me as we walked was that I needed to slow down. Up to this point Father Joe and I rarely took breaks. We would stop to get water or pray, but we didn't take off our shoes and relax.

I remember one afternoon when, on a sloped grass yard of a small nameless church, the three of us took a ninety-minute break. This was unheard of: What a waste of time! We took off our shoes, talked, ate, laughed and rolled on the grassy hill. We took crazy pictures of one another stretching aching muscles, and we laughed a lot more. It was one of the best breaks of the Camino.

After our extended break Father Joe and I were ready to pray the rosary. We did this at least once a day and often more. We told Mara that if we were going to walk together, she would have to learn to pray the rosary. So as we walked we taught her the meaning of the rosary and how to pray it. It seemed to me that she genuinely enjoyed the experience. For me there was something beautiful about the three of us walking down a dusty Spanish road praying the rosary together.

This day would turn out to be one of the longest days. We began walking at 7:00 in the morning and were not finished till 6:45 PM, having walked over twenty-two miles. When we arrived at the albergue, there was no room in the inn, so to speak, so we ended up sleeping on mattresses in one of the hallways. After such a long day, we were grateful for this.

The next day the three of us stopped for lunch in Santo Domingo de la Calzada. For several days I had been looking for the walking staff that was going to accompany me for the Camino, and Santo Domingo was a good-size town, so I went looking for my staff.

I guess my main reason for wanting a staff was because it was part of the tradition of being a pilgrim on the Camino. For centuries pilgrims have carried staffs to aid their walk but also for numerous practical purposes, such as keeping wild animals at bay. I also like the image of Jesus as the shepherd, and walking with a shepherd's staff was one of my desires.

Oh, and one more thing: A staff looks cool.

After lunch I stopped by a little wood shop near the church of Santo Domingo and found the perfect pilgrim's staff. At last I was finished accessorizing; I now looked the pilgrim's part.

It was here that I had to say good-bye to Mara, since Father Joe and I were on a tighter schedule than she was and had to continue walking. I left Santo Domingo asking God what he wanted me to learn from my time with her. By her own admission Mara was only recently beginning to follow God more seriously, and it seemed she was trying to work out some fundamental aspects of her faith. I found myself thinking a lot about her and praying a great deal for her.

Love One Another

My time with Mara made it clear to me that I was not supposed to try to convince her of something or of some way of believing. Sometimes I think that, rather than really trying to know another person, especially one very different from myself, I can't get past my agenda of what I want to happen. I want the person to change so badly that I fail to recognize the beauty of the person. Jesus didn't treat people like this.

Throughout my entire time with Mara, I felt God asking me to walk with her and be present to her. In the end God was calling me to love. This is what I tried to do. And the experience was transformative.

I don't think I am that different from a lot of people. How often we look for what we think should be rather than for the beauty that is. We forget that the person in front of us is deeply loved by God, and that this is what matters most. What a tragedy really, because there is so much we can learn and so much splendor in people different from ourselves.

I heard Jesus' words reverberating in my heart: "Dave, did you love the way I loved?" I think of the story of Jesus and the woman at the well (see John 4). There was no judgment, no condemnation, just love, just mercy.

I can't be sure if I learned this lesson completely or not, but it will always stay with me and will be one of the lasting impressions of my Camino. Can I love for love's sake? Can I love without expecting anything in return but only for the sake of love? Something radically changes in our spiritual lives when we are able to love in this way.

In the end I cherished my time with Mara, what she taught me and what I learned. What a blessing to be on the Camino.

I almost forgot: My feet were still killing me.

7 : LET IT END!

I thought I was in good shape. For the month before the Camino I trained, and I believed that I was about as prepared to go as I could be. I suppose I could have walked a little more and carried my pack a few more times, but at this moment in the Camino I didn't think any of that would have mattered. Having thought more about my training, I had come to realize that I went about it all wrong. The long walks by myself up and down hills were not the right way to get ready.

In order to prepare properly, I would have had to acquire the help of another person. His job would have been instrumental in my being prepared to walk the Camino. Every day for, say, twenty or thirty minutes, maybe longer on weekends, I would have had to lie on my back with my shoes and socks off. Then my partner would have hit the bottoms of my feet as hard as he possibly could with a meat mallet. Only after a month or so of training such as this would I have been prepared for what I was going to feel while walking the Camino.

I was honestly taken aback at how sore my feet were. I had reasoned that the discomfort could not be as bad as people said. I walk all the time, and my feet rarely hurt. I was sure they were all exaggerating.

I was wrong; they were right. It *could* be as bad as they said. My feet hurt; they hurt a lot.

And if misery loves company, I had lots of company.

Pain Afoot

It was quite a sight at the end of the day to watch everyone walking around the albergue—if you can call what we were doing walking; hobbling may be a better word. In a very sick and twisted way, it was at times rather comical. We looked as if we were walking barefoot on a path riddled with glass and sharp pebbles. Each step was calculated and carefully planned: step, stop, step, stop.

The first thing I would do when I arrived at an albergue was peel off my shoes and lie on my bed. I would place my sleeping bag under my feet so that they would be elevated. These were treasured moments. I would simply lie there and contemplate whether or not I really needed a shower or bathroom or food. At that moment all bets were off; everything was optional.

Eventually it would become clear to me that I had to move. It would be a rare albergue that offered sponge baths or dinner in bed, so I had to get up.

On one such occasion I staggered down a flight of stairs, holding on to the handrail as if my life depended on it, cursing the inventor of stairs. I encountered a young woman sputtering her way up. Our eyes met, and we started laughing. What a sight we were.

Our sleeping quarters often looked like a M.A.S.H. unit. Everyone would sit at the edge of the bed caring for feet as well as other problem spots. The floor would be littered with adhesive bandage packages, as the familiar odor of BENGAY wafted through the room.

Everyone had his or her own way of dealing with blisters. This ranged from poking them with a needle (I have not seen so many needles in one place since I was last in my grandmother's sewing room) to letting them burst on their own. Each person was convinced that his or her method was best, only to try something different the next day.

I was thankful to not have any blisters at this time. This was a blessing because blisters would have added insult to injury. Father Joe, however, was not so lucky. He had several blisters and had decided that desperate times called for desperate measures.

We had heard that one way to make the blisters heal faster was to take a needle and thread, place the needle through the blister and then leave the thread dangling out either side. The theory was that the blister would drain, dry out and heal much faster. There were several pilgrims trying this method, so Father Joe figured he would give it a shot.

I must say that Father Joe's foot, with thread hanging out on either side, looked remotely like an old, tattered Raggedy Andy doll. But he was willing to give just about anything a try.

Later, when I shared the details of this procedure with my father, who is a physician, he felt that this was a really bad idea. It sounded to him like a great way to get an infection. Of course, he wasn't there. Mercifully Father Joe did not get any infections.

It was important that I not miss the opportunity for grace. I told myself repeatedly that all the discomfort I was experiencing was "for the King." Everything I experienced and everything I was going through, I wanted to offer in thanksgiving to God for allowing me to be a priest.

I want to be clear: While my pain and discomfort of swollen feet and a weary body were real, compared to what many people have to deal with on a daily basis, my situation was rather insignificant. But I did find myself reflecting on how people would think that I was crazy to put myself through all of this. "Why would you choose to do this?" Believe me, that is a great question and one that I asked myself time and time again.

There were times when the only thing I could focus on was my discomfort, and because of this I totally missed the beauty around me and lacked sensitivity to my fellow pilgrims. All I was looking at was myself. However, this provided a wonderful revelation.

It occurred to me that some people are so full of pain that they are not able to see the beauty around them. They hurt so badly that all they can think about is their hurt. It is not that they are selfish or lack sensitivity; it's just that their pain is consuming.

This experience has helped me be much more patient with others. Where in the past I would get frustrated, I think I am able now to be more loving. I really don't know what is going on in another person's heart, and I don't know the pain others are going through. I pray for the grace to not judge others.

Freely Chosen

I began to contemplate the fact that I had freely chosen the Camino. No one made me do it, and no one was making me get up each day and continue walking. I could have stopped, and my discomfort would have ended. But I kept on.

This caused me to think about a text from John's Gospel. In John 10:17–18 Jesus states that no one takes his life from him, but he freely chooses to lay it down. This humbled me. Jesus freely chose to give his life for me. In the midst of his pain and suffering, at any moment he could have said, "Enough," but he didn't. Rather he endured the cross for me (see Hebrews 12:2).

Because of Jesus' freely choosing suffering, I am able to pursue holiness. It was his pain that healed the wounds of my sin. I feel so incredibly inadequate, so insignificant, so limited. Jesus, how can I ever thank you?

And his cross was not just for me: Jesus bore the weight of sin for all humanity. "He himself bore our sins in his body on the tree, that we might die to sin and live to righteousness. By his wounds you have been healed" (1 Peter 2:24).

I experienced something beautiful in my lowly offering. The pain I was experiencing was a choice that I had made and continued to make. And in the midst of it all, I experienced a profound presence of Christ in my offering.

Many people experience a great deal of suffering due to things that are beyond their control, and I know that God desires to show himself to those people. I know many moving stories of people who have offered their suffering for the glory of God. But in my case I was freely choosing this discomfort and freely choosing to experience it for my King. I began to understand more why God had invited me to walk the Camino. "For to this you have been called, because Christ also suffered for you, leaving you an example that you should follow in his steps" (1 Peter 2:21). Has there ever been a Scripture so appropriate at a given time?

God was revealing to me a particular beauty in this self-donation. There was a part of the inconvenience of sore feet and an aching body that actually became sweet, transcending my human discomfort and allowing me to briefly be touched by the divine. I was beginning to understand more fully the power in offering simple sacrifices for the Lord.

Fasting for a day isn't simply giving up food in order to lose a pound or two. Rather it is freely choosing to be uncomfortable, if only for a brief time, so that God can share with me the transforming beauty of offering myself for something greater.

God invites us to offer him everything—everything! There are many opportunities in our day for grace, but so often we miss them by whining and complaining. Imagine offering your frustration at your kids or spouse to Jesus. Or when waking up tired or sick and, rather than complaining, uniting that feeling to Jesus. Or instead of getting angry with the person in front of you who has fifteen items in the twelve-item lane, praying for the person or praying that you can be more patient.

These may seem like minor, meaningless things, but I believe they have a great impact on our spiritual lives. Jesus invites us to unite all we are to him, to go to him with everything. When we are able to give him everything, especially the junk, he is able to radically change us. This is pure gift.

8 : LESSONS IN WALKING

You learn a lot when you get up day after day and walk. It's funny; it is something that most of us take for granted. From the days when we take our first steps, till we grow older and find the task more difficult, we just don't think a lot about walking. Sadly, some of the most precious things in life we take for granted.

I usually woke up around six o'clock without any kind of alarm. Some people preferred to get up and get going at around five, long before the sun rose. Whatever winds their watch, but this didn't appeal to me for two main reasons.

First—and I could actually stop here—it was 5:00 AM. Second, I did not like getting ready in the dark. I tried it once early in the pilgrimage, and it just didn't appeal to me. I didn't like getting dressed, sorting through my stuff and packing my sleeping bag while holding the flashlight steady in my mouth. Nope. Give me another hour in bed, let the sun rise and get where it was meant to be, and then I will get up and begin walking.

Walking each day taught me many things. One of the blessings of the Camino is that you have the time to let God teach you about really simple, beautiful things.

The Right Path
One of the things that I had quickly learned on the Camino was that the surface that you walk on makes all the difference in the

world. In the past I had never really paid much attention to the surface under my feet. However, when you are walking seven or eight hours a day, you don't take anything for granted, especially when it comes to your feet.

The walk this particular day was just over seventeen miles, which was not terribly long. For about thirteen miles I walked on a soft dirt trail, which was generally the surface of choice. Near the end of this section, my feet were beginning to be pretty sore, but they were about to get much worse.

The path changed from a nice, luxurious dirt path to evil concrete. It appears that the people of Logroño, our stopping place for the day, wanted to give a gift to the pilgrims, and they created a "beautiful concrete path" in order to welcome pilgrims into their lovely town. While I appreciated the gesture, I think I would have preferred trees to shade me from the hot sun.

After walking thirteen miles, finishing the last four on hard concrete was miserable. (All this for the King, I know, I know.)

One of my fellow pilgrims questioned, "Do you think the fine people of this lovely hamlet would consider a foot massage instead of the concrete path?" It is worth noting that the guidebook I was using mentioned that Logroño had a fine hospital able to treat foot and leg problems. Coincidence?

When I prayed at the end of the day, I was reminded of a Scripture from Matthew (see Matthew 7:13-14). Jesus said that there is a path that looks great: It is wide and flat, but it ultimately leads to death. The other path is more rugged, but it leads to life. We can't just choose the path that looks the easiest. The concrete path looked great, and at first it appeared to be easy, but ultimately it was a killer.

I have got to stay on the narrow path that leads to life. Even though this path at times will be difficult, God has promised to be with us every step of the way. I love Psalm 119:105, "Your word is a lamp to my feet and a light to my path." I am continually struck by the fact that the psalm does not say that God is a light all the way down the road but rather "a lamp to my feet and a light to my path." How often I want God to light the way to the end. But he chooses not to work that way.

He is a lamp to our feet. The next step I take, I will be able to see. I won't stumble or fall, because the lamp will shed enough light that I will be able to take a steady step. This is true for the next step as well. And the next. And the next. I need to claim this and pray that I will know and believe this to be true.

God is going to take care of us, whether or not we can see down the road. He will not let us walk in darkness and leave us there alone. He will not let us walk to a place and abandon us.

> He leads me in paths of righteousness
>> for his name's sake.
> Even though I walk through the valley of the shadow of
>> death,
>> I fear no evil;
> for you are with me;
>> your rod and your staff
>> they comfort me. (Psalm 23:3–4)

Slow but Steady

If you pay attention you can learn a lot when you are walking. One morning as I was climbing over an old stone fence, I noticed a snail sitting (do snails sit?) on one of the rocks. Given that I had a lot of time on my feet, I found myself thinking about the snail. I can't say that I had ever thought about the life of a snail, nor had I ever compared myself to a snail, but while on the Camino one does lots of things that one has not previously done.

Everyone has heard the term *a snail's pace*. A snail is not going to break any speed records: it moves ahead very, very slowly. But if it keeps moving forward, it will eventually get where it wants to go.

And so was my life on the Camino.

And so is the spiritual life.

This particular day was a short one, only about thirteen miles. When I thought of how little I had walked, it seemed like a waste of time: "This is going to take me forever; at this pace the slimy snail is going to get to Santiago before me."

It did occur to me, however, that over time, if I went thirteen miles a day, I would end up covering a lot of ground. And what was ultimately most important was that I progressed forward. I did not quit. I did not turn around. I kept moving ahead, even at what seemed like a snail's pace.

The spiritual life is just that: a life. In order to progress we must renew our commitment to Christ daily and then be committed to doing this over and over again. It is a lot like walking the Camino: Just keep moving forward.

"Jesus, I want to love you today and be loved by you today. Help me to do better than I did yesterday."

This is an essential part of the spiritual life: steady progress day after day. While there are seasons when we progress more quickly, I don't believe they are the norm; rather they are special moments of grace. They soon will fade, and we will be back to the faithful, daily growth.

The author of Hebrews put it well: "You have need of endurance, so that you may do the will of God and receive what is promised" (Hebrews 10:36).

Many people who are becoming more serious about the spiritual life need to be more patient with themselves. I know many who want to be at the end (perfectly holy) right away, and it simply does not work that way. They need to take an honest assessment of where they are and make a commitment to move forward.

While keeping the end goal in mind, they must take steps daily in order to get there. Faithfulness is key to really growing in the spiritual life. We are not perfect, but we keep on going even when we fall. Mother Teresa always spoke of "faithfulness, not success," and this is all the more impressive in light of the fact that she went over forty years without any sense of God's consolation.

Each day we get up in the morning and choose to love better than we did the previous day. This is growth in the spiritual life.

I Have to Win

I admit that there were times when going at a snail's pace was not easy for me. Maybe this is because I am kind of competitive.

Don't get me wrong: I don't think that is necessarily a bad thing. Competition can be good in the proper context. In fact, it can produce great character in a person. But taken too far or in different situations, it can be a bad thing. On the Camino and in the spiritual life, it can be a real problem.

One particular morning started no differently from any other. We began walking at around 7:30, while the sun was burning off a light morning haze. My body felt good, and I was walking at a fairly quick clip. Then, seemingly out of nowhere, a couple of pilgrims took the inside of a sharp curve and blew right past me. I hadn't even seen them coming.

It was pathetic how this affected me. I actually got frustrated that I had been passed. "If we hadn't have stopped to go to the bathroom, we would still be ahead of them." I decided that I needed to walk faster and take the lead once again. There was no way that I was going to get passed.

It was not long before I was forced to accept defeat. Those other people had won. They walked faster and were the "better" pilgrims. I licked my wounds and assured myself that it was really OK. I had passed a lot of other pilgrims, so I was quicker than most.

What is crazy is that I am not *totally* exaggerating. (Be honest, does it ever bug you when you get passed on the highway?) I knew that this was ridiculous.

God used this event. In fact, it became a real moment of grace for me.

When I was praying later that evening, I found myself reflecting on my feelings about getting passed. Why did it bother me? For goodness' sake, I was on a pilgrimage, not in a race. This was not a competition, I reminded myself.

Or was it? Or more accurately, had I made it one?

Perhaps deep inside of me, a part of me that I was embarrassed about, I had made it into a competition. I felt God telling me that it did not matter if I finished first: it wasn't about "winning." All that mattered was that I was walking and that I would finish. My fellow pilgrims were certainly not my competition; rather they were my brothers and sisters.

In our desire to grow in the spiritual life, we are not in competition with one another. While Saint Paul does use the imagery of a race (see 1 Corinthians 9:25), he does not say that our brothers and sisters are the competition. I do not become holy at your expense, and your growing in virtue takes nothing away from me. On the contrary, I actually can be more converted if I can help you grow.

In the end it is about my being faithful, responding to what God has asked me to do and praying that my brothers and sisters will have the same grace. It is not about my being better, faster or holier than others.

What God asks another person to do has no bearing on what he asks of me. All that I want is to know what Jesus is asking of me and the grace to say yes to that.

I have heard it said that purgatory is full of people who did *more* than God asked of them. I want to do only what Jesus asks me to do. If he wants me to walk more slowly, and God forbid, I get passed in the process, bless God, as long as I am walking as he desires.

Another day on the Camino, another day closer to God.

9 : THANKS A LOT

I love being a priest. I can't imagine doing anything else, and I am grateful that God invited me to this vocation. The very reason I chose to do the Camino was to thank him for that.

Priesthood was the topic of another long day.

There was nothing out of the ordinary or particularly unique about the day's walk. Every now and then Father Joe and I would just pick a topic and talk. Sometimes the topic was our favorite birthday, favorite athletic team or most memorable girlfriend. But today the topic was priesthood. It was a lot of fun walking along the Camino path and remembering how I got there.

I don't remember a time when the thought of being a priest was not in my mind. My parents prayed from the beginning of their married life that one of their children would have a religious vocation. With five boys and one girl in my family, the odds were looking good.

Knowing of my parents' desire, my brothers and I gathered in the kitchen and pulled straws: Short one becomes a priest. I won, or lost, depending on whom and when you ask.

My parents tell of a time when a priest was visiting our home and asked me what I wanted to do when I grew up. I stated that I wanted to be a priest. My parents go on to say that if he had been a teacher, I would have said I wanted to be a teacher, or if he was a pilot ... you get the point.

Perhaps this is why, early in college, I was in the prelaw program and interested in politics. I pursued this path for about two years but still had a nagging feeling that God was calling me to something different.

The Desire of My Heart

It was at that time that I heard of the National Evangelization Teams (NET), which is an evangelistic ministry based in Saint Paul, Minnesota. I thought this would be a great way to serve the Church as well as give me some time to discern my call. I applied and was accepted.

I loved my time with NET, and the depth of the call to the priesthood increased. After my year of service, I was fairly certain that God did want me to be a priest, and I transferred to Franciscan University in Steubenville, Ohio, in order to finish my education.

During my college years I spent a great deal of time praying about the deepest desire of my heart. Psalm 37:4 speaks of God fulfilling the desires of the heart, and I prayed that I would know without question what that desire was for me. I had long given my heart to Christ, and I believed that he was going to lead me and help me discern his will. However, coming to fully understand the desires of the human heart is not always easy.

I believe that I was totally open to whatever God wanted. "Lord, tell me what you want of me, and I will gladly do it."

And then one day God said to me, "Dave, give up that which you want to know for the one who wants to tell you." These were some of the most freeing words I have ever heard God speak. They changed the way I approached God then and continue to affect the way I seek him now.

I realized that I had been going after what God wanted rather than going after God. Christ was inviting me to surrender what I wanted to know and simply seek him, seek his face, listen to his voice. Jesus was inviting me to a deeper union with him. And it was there, nearer to his heart, that I would discover his will for me.

His will was not a riddle that I had to figure out. It was not a matter of talking with the right person or reading the perfect book or article to find exactly what God wanted of me. Rather, I would discover his will by peering deeply into his eyes and seeing his love and passion for me.

At that moment I decided I would stop the constant prayer about my vocation. No longer would it dominate my prayer time; rather I would seek Christ and ask to fall in love with him more. I would dedicate Saturday mornings to only spiritual reading and prayer related to the priesthood.

From that moment on my discernment process became much more peaceful. However, there were other issues.

Holy Choices

My reason for becoming a priest was not that I did not want to get married. My mom and dad were wonderful examples of a Catholic, Christian marriage, and I had witnessed in them the beauty of marriage and found this to be very attractive. But at the same time I had a pull toward the priesthood. This bewildered me. How was this possible to want both when both were not possible?

From my reading, spiritual direction and a lot of prayer, I came to understand something vitally important to discernment. Authentic discernment is always between two goods. I didn't have to discern whether I should be a priest or a drug dealer: This was self-evident. Rather I had to discern between two things that are both good. This being the case, having an attraction to both was perfectly normal.

What this meant for me was that if I were to discern that I should be a priest, then I would have to say no to the beautiful good that is marriage. This helped me make sense of why I would have a kind of sadness when I spoke or thought of not getting married. It was not that I didn't want to be a priest, because really I did; it was only that I was saying no to something beautiful, and for a while this caused me to feel down and confused. Once I understood this I experienced much more peace.

Another breakthrough came one day when I was sitting in a theology class. The professor spoke passionately of the call that each baptized Christian has to be holy. This was God's call for our lives. Holiness was his will for *me*!

I felt like Saint Francis when he heard God's call to leave behind everything and follow God. My heart cried out, "Yes, this is what I want, this is what I long for, this is what I desire with all my heart."

Holiness had been a central part of my prayer, but I had not really connected it to God's call for my life. Yes, God wanted me to be holy; that was the bottom line. However, I wondered if I could really be called to be a priest because I was fully aware that I was, in fact, not holy. I had so many things to work on and so much pride and selfishness that had to be rooted out of my life.

But as I reflected on the call to be holy, it became clear to me that God had a pattern of calling "nonholy" people to follow and serve him. I thought of David in the Old Testament, Peter, Paul and Mary Magdalene in the New Testament and Francis. There was nothing particularly holy about these people, but they became holy. And I thought about me. Seriously, I don't think I would have called me. Believe me, I know me, and I'm really not that impressive.

Then it hit me: It was the *call* that made those people holy. God calls ordinary individuals to follow him, and by their yes to this call, God proceeds to make them holy. To the degree that I surrender all to follow Jesus, he really can make me holy.

From there I had to continue to think and pray about what vocation would allow me to be holiest. Obviously, for me it was the priesthood. But this was *my* call. I see my brothers and sister with their children and fully believe that that is how God is making them holy. There is no doubt in my mind that being awoken five times in a night to children throwing up has the possibility of being transformative. Dealing with this situation in love, kindness and tenderness is supernatural.

There was one other significant event. Again I was in prayer, this time in the Portiuncula, a replica on the Steubenville campus of the chapel closest to Saint Francis's heart. By this time I was relatively certain that God wanted me to be a priest. I asked God if this was indeed his will, to give me the perseverance that it would take.

While I was praying this, I felt God ask me "to bear the fruit that must endure; it *must* endure." There was a real sense of urgency and necessity in the way God spoke. The fruit must endure!

It was clear to me that God was inviting me to be a priest and that my vocation must endure. It was also obvious that I now had to decide how I would respond to God's call.

Just Say Yes

The final step took place on a bench next to the road that leads to the Franciscan campus. I was sitting there with one of the friars, and I told him that I believed that God wanted me to be a priest and that I wanted to be a priest. I was expecting the clouds to open and to hear trumpets blasts and a voice from the heavens stating that I was his son and he was well pleased. Nothing. But what I did have was peace. I had said yes, and in the deepest parts of my heart I was at peace.

In the end I believe that peace is ultimately how we know what God is asking of us. I have never received an e-mail from God telling me what he wanted me to do. But I have experienced his peace, and I believe that this is the normal way God confirms his will for me. This is not to say that this doesn't need to be tested, but a peace that is deeper than I can explain is a good indication of what God wants me to do. I do my best to seek his will and then take a step in faith that God is with me.

I struggle to express in words the gratitude I feel toward God for the call to be a priest. Perhaps this is why I chose to walk across Spain.

I am so blessed to be a priest. At the beginning of every Mass I celebrate, when I venerate the altar, I say, "Thank you, Jesus, for allowing me to be a priest." And when I genuflect at the time of consecration, I say, "Jesus, where would I be had you not intervened in my life? Thank you."

I know that I am not worthy to be a priest and that I fail often. This is not some false humility but absolute truth. However, God in his love and mercy has invited me to love him and be loved by him as a priest. He chose me; it was not I who chose him, and he chose me to bear fruit that must endure (see John 15:16). He has invited me to lay down my life for him and with him and shepherd his people, and for this I am eternally thankful.

10 : COME TO THE TABLE

From the beginning I was told that your body adjusts after ten days, and then it is not so bad. I think that is all a conspiracy to get people to go on the Camino. If people thought the entire walk was going to be pain and misery, they would never do it. So you tell them it will only hurt for "about ten days." And by day ten of the Camino, they have invested too much to turn around.

Well, it had been twelve days, and my body still hurt. I had walked about 170 miles and felt almost every one of them. I could not get out of my mind the words of a woman I had met on the second or third day. She was walking the Camino for the second time, and I asked her when the pain would go away. She declared in a raspy smoker's voice, "The pain never goes away."

Wonderful.

When we stopped in San Juan de Ortega, I honestly was frustrated. While I had to admit that the days were getting better and my body was not hurting as badly as earlier in the walk, this day had been a tough one. I had walked about twenty-four miles, and because of the hills it had been a pretty grueling day.

An elderly man with very dark weathered skin checked me in at the albergue. He asked how far I had walked, and when I told him, he whistled and confirmed in broken English, "Long day, big long day." Tell me about it.

Mass and Dinner

I was discouraged. I lay down on my bed and tried to rest but only grew more disheartened. I wrote in my journal of my frustration. Maybe that "ten day" thing was branded in my mind, and I was disappointed that my body was still sore. Maybe I was just tired. But I had been very tired before and not felt so down.

Perhaps the real problem had nothing to do with my body being sore or being tired. There was a church connected to the albergue, so I went there to pray and get ready for Mass. It was a Sunday, and Father Joe and I were excited to be part of a larger community for the liturgy.

I was quite surprised to see that the priest presiding at Mass was the old weathered man who had checked me in at the albergue. He had a very gentle and loving presence about him. And while I did not understand most of what he said, there was something comforting in the familiarity of the liturgy.

The small stone Gothic church was so full of pilgrims that men and women were sitting on the floor in the aisles. It was pretty obvious that a large percentage were not Catholic. However, there was clearly a sense of community and unity among all attending Mass that evening.

The next stop was dinner, and this could not come too soon. The albergue did not have a kitchen, so we ate at the small place next door. I ordered the pilgrim's meal and waited to see what was going to come.

First was a wonderful salad, which was a nice change of pace. I couldn't remember the last salad I had eaten. The main course was pork chops, with fried potatoes and maybe squash. Everything tasted wonderful.

An Anglican priest from Cambridge joined Father Joe and me for dinner. We shared a bottle of red wine and enjoyed each other's company. We chatted about the Church in England and shared our vocation stories. The meal was topped off with some kind of Spanish pastry, a perfect finish to a satisfying meal.

When I went back to my room to journal and pray more, I found that I felt totally different. I was no longer frustrated, and in fact I felt strangely peaceful and content. What had changed?

It was the meal–both of them.

Food for the Journey

On the night before Jesus died, he gathered his disciples together for a meal. He could have brought them together for one last conference: "OK, I need to remind you of a few things and make absolutely certain you understand the following points." But he didn't. They gathered for a meal.

The meal was familiar and nonthreatening. It satisfied the physical needs of the body, which cannot be underestimated, but it did so much more than that. Meals are important.

I have many fond memories of meals. Given that I have a large family, the evening meal was a pretty big undertaking. We all had our assigned places, or at least our customary places. I don't know that these were actually assigned, but no one would ever think of taking someone else's place.

This was an important time in our household. We would pray and talk about our day. I remember laughing a lot, especially one Thanksgiving when someone dropped the turkey on the kitchen floor though, if I recall correctly, Mom did not think it was too funny. These were great times.

Many families don't eat together anymore, which is terribly unfortunate. Studies indicate that children who regularly eat with their families have fewer social and discipline problems. It's just good for you! I hear people say they are too busy, but I think we are never too busy for priorities.

My family would also go to Sunday Mass together at 11:00 AM. I remember as a little boy having my clothes set out for Sunday Mass and having my older brothers help me and my younger brothers get ready. I am sure that this was often a hectic time for my parents, but reflecting back yields wonderful memories.

As we had our assigned seats at dinner, our family had our assigned place at Mass. The second pew on the right was the "Pivonka Pew." I don't know why it was, it just was. With the exception of an unaware summer tourist, no one else would sit in the "Pivonka Pew."

Sunday Mass brings back many fond memories. I recall asking Mom and Dad after Communion if we had been good enough to get donuts. Then there was the time my youngest brother ran up the center aisle holding the nipple of his bottle and banging every pew. Or the time when I was serving and fell asleep, banging my head on the altar—no most valuable server award that year!

Then there were the times when something happened that caused one of us to start laughing, and the laughter became contagious. There is nothing more difficult in the world than to stop laughing in the middle of church.

I also recall watching my mom cry during the consecration and knowing that something pretty amazing was happening. My mind is stamped with the image of my father kneeling down in prayer with his face buried in his hands. I recall siblings' confirmations and Easter Vigils, which always ended in desserts at a local restaurant.

How blessed I was to attend Mass with my family. Those times were formative for me. Most obviously, there was never any question in my mind that Mass was a part of Sunday.

I am sure there were many times when my parents were frustrated on Sunday morning. I am certain that getting six kids ready for Mass was at times a struggle. I would guess that oftentimes Mass was not the most prayerful experience for my parents. But we always went.

Mass was not merely an important or a good thing to do; rather it was essential. I never recall a conversation regarding going to Mass or not. Just as dinner was a part of our life, so was Mass.

I was reminded of this on the Camino. That evening in San Juan del Ortega, I experienced the beauty of both meals and began to see them both differently.

Both feed the body and the soul. Jesus in his self-offering feeds me so that I am able to live the life to which he has called me. In the Eucharist my eternal soul is fed; it is satisfied with the only food that can satisfy, the Eternal One himself. I come to his table weary, broken and ragged, and he heals me, he feeds me, and he makes me whole.

The meal following the Mass also had a great effect on me. It provided my body sustenance as well as enlivening my spirit. The conversation with Father Joe and a fellow pilgrim was transformative. Sharing a glass of wine while listening to one another's stories was beautiful.

After my long day of walking, I was grateful for the many ways God reveals himself to me, especially in holy meals. Because of this experience and others, I love meals for the graced moments they offer.

11 : MAKE ME CLEAN

Men and women are different. I would guess that this is not an earth-shattering revelation to anyone. I suppose it is a part of God's eternal sense of humor that men and women marry and are then to live in the same house and sleep in the same bed "till death do them part."

One time I was taking a graduate class, and the topic was the differences between men and women. The professor explained that, other than biological, there are no real differences between men and women, and asserted that all differences are thrust upon us by culture. "We give baby boys blue blankets and girls pink."

The professor then expounded on how we should raise all children without any stereotypical, cultural, sexual, biases, and then children would be free to determine for themselves if they were male or female. Well, that's an interesting idea. But as a nine-year-old son of my friend stated, "That's stupid, Father Dave"—out of the mouths of babes.

The point is that men and women are different; they just are. It's always been that way and will always be.

This was very evident on the Camino. I remember a group of Italian girls who, on their first day, were up early doing their hair and makeup, which led to an unusually long amount of time in front of the mirror. The cute little red polka-dot ribbons in their hair matched their shirts, shorts and socks. Meanwhile, most of the men were not even aware that there was a mirror and were not that concerned if their shorts matched their socks. Simply having shorts on was a real step forward for some.

It should be noted, however, that by day four or five these same Italian girls had become much less concerned about whether their ribbons matched their shorts. They were more concerned about surviving another day.

Dirty Laundry

I guess I noticed one of the greatest differences between men and women when it came time to wash my clothes. There were typically washbasins in the courtyard, and as pilgrims arrived they would gather to do their wash. Given that most of us only had two outfits (I have a little trouble calling what I wore an outfit, but you get the point), it would be necessary each day to wash one of them.

So pilgrims would wait their turns at the washbasins and talk about the day's walk. This was a really pleasurable part of the day.

The tools for washing were pretty rustic in most places. Usually we had an old washboard or rock and a faucet. I don't recall ever having warm water. There was often a bar of soap at the basin, which I would use as my detergent. If there was no soap there, I would use my own. Yes, it is true, the same soap I washed my body with I would also use for my clothes. Don't judge me; you weren't there.

I became somewhat enamored with the difference between how many of the women washed clothes and how I washed mine. It was like the difference between a gourmet chef and the guy who cooks the hot dogs behind the counter at a corner gas station.

You see, washing my clothes took maybe four minutes. I would turn the water on, get the clothes wet, rub some soap on them, rinse most of the soap out and, in one fluid motion, "wring and hang." A few well-placed safety pins to secure them to the line, and I was good to go.

There was a science to how some of the women washed. First off, is it really necessary to sort your clothes if you are washing them in a basin? OK, let's be honest: Is it *ever* necessary to sort your clothes?

These women were unbelievably meticulous. They would first clean the basin—a wasted step if you ask me. They would then fill the basin with water, add some type of detergent and get the water all sudsy. They would plunge a piece of clothing into the water and pull it out, repeating this several times with a motion that strongly resembled that of a man working a jackhammer.

They would take the item entirely out of the water, grab it by the edges and quickly rub the fabric together. They then stretched their arms out, gazed at the garment and repeated the entire process. I am fairly certain that a couple of times I saw sparks and smoke during this stage of the wash cycle.

Mind you, this was no short ritual. I could be well into the fourth mystery of the rosary before they were even thinking about the rinse cycle.

It was now time to empty the basin and refill it for the above-mentioned rinse cycle. I have to say that this was another wasted step that had never crossed my mind.

The rinse cycle looked vaguely like the wash cycle and was done with every bit as much energy and tenacity. I could only figure that these women had not walked as far as I had, given the vigor with which they washed their clothes. I was breaking a sweat just watching.

The final stage was the "wringing out" cycle. As I mentioned previously, I had merged the rinse cycle and the wringing out cycle into one fluid motion. (No doubt I was the slacker of the Camino when it came to washing.) By the time these women had wrung out their clothes, they clearly could have skipped the drying stage, which I might add was my personal favorite. There was no more excess water in those clothes than there is in the middle of the Mojave Desert.

But they did hang the clothes neatly on the line, and then they would step back, place their hands on their hips and admire their work. I am sure that each one of them experienced a sense of pride and accomplishment to which, given the task, I simply was unable to relate.

Purify Me

I found myself mildly obsessed with this washing ritual. I continued to reflect on it while walking. And in a moment of brilliance, I realized something quite profound.

The objective or goal of the women's washing was quite different from mine. They washed to get their clothes clean. I had to admit that this was not necessarily my end goal. I only wanted to make sure that my clothes didn't stink. A big difference.

I was quite satisfied with my ability to recognize the distinction between our two methods of washing. But this led to a startling thought. I realized that a lot of the time when I repent for my sin and go to confession, it is not because I truly want to be clean; rather it is because I don't want to "stink" anymore. I don't want to feel guilty or feel bad.

Sadly, I fear, I have often used confession as a "quick rinse cycle." I go before God, repent of my sin and in some way feel as if I have done what is expected of me. But oftentimes, if I were to be totally honest with myself, I did not go to confession so that I would be clean or pure but just so that I could stand myself and not stink. I was struck to the heart.

I knew this to be true, and I also knew that I was not alone. I can see it among people who come to me for confession. There are those who read off a grocery list of sins and others who really understand how they have offended God and with all their heart do not want to hurt him again. It is the difference between "Bless me, Father, for I did x, y and z" and "Bless me, Father, for I have broken God's heart."

There is a profound difference between approaching God because *I* feel bad or guilty and going before the one whom I have offended, the one who loves me perfectly, and saying I am sorry for breaking his heart. In one case I am at the center; in the other it is God.

Don't get me wrong: It is always good to repent before God. This is never a bad thing, but there is more. I believe one type of repentance is motivated by love, and the other by guilt, fear, superstition or any number of things. When I repent before God, I truly desire to present myself to him so that he can make me clean. I also long to have a firm conviction to not sin again.

I hope that I never use the confessional as a "quick wash" cycle, without remembering what Jesus did that allowed me to be forgiven. I want to approach the sacrament with a radical awareness that confession is a result of Jesus' death. I pray that, when I go to confession, I am motivated to be pure and clean, the same way some of my fellow pilgrims were motivated to actually wash their clothes.

12 : HOME AWAY FROM HOME

Choosing the right albergue is very important. Most of the villages I stayed in had a choice of a couple of albergues, and I had a few driving principles when choosing my crib for the night.

Whenever possible I chose an albergue that had lots of rooms and only a few beds in each room. While for the most part I enjoyed my fellow pilgrims, sleeping with a hundred of them was more enjoyment than I could stand. I tried to stay in the private albergues rather than the public ones, which usually lacked any type of personality.

Father Joe and I had also decided that we wanted to cook, so a kitchen was important. However, as the Camino went on, we got lazy and cooked less. We found we really enjoyed participating in the pilgrims' meals at local diners, and toward the end we opted for these quite a bit.

Showers were also very important, but there was not a lot of planning you could do about this. Every albergue had some kind of shower, but several of them were simply hoses in a type of water closet. I would say that over the entire Camino, about 85 percent of my showers were cold. I am not good at cold showers, so this was a time of conversion for me.

It was a real plus if I could stay in an albergue that had a nice courtyard. The courtyard was a great gathering place. In the afternoons and evenings, pilgrims from around the world would sit there and talk, tell stories and commiserate about their pain.

Time spent hanging out in the various albergues was one of the most enjoyable parts of the Camino.

I remember with great fondness the courtyard in Astorga. There were lots of tables and chairs, and the space was loaded with various kinds of plants and trees. But the most memorable aspect was a type of water trough with little benches and buckets that ran along one side of the courtyard. Pilgrims sat there with their feet in the water. The buckets contained a type of salt that the pilgrims put in the water; it was supposed to be therapeutic.

I didn't know if the saltwater actually made a difference, but heck, at that point I would have soaked my feet in monkey spit if it had held any promise to make them feel better. So I soaked my feet for about fifteen minutes, and I had to admit they did not hurt anymore. However, this might have been due to the fact that my feet had become numb knobs, since the water was absolutely frigid.

While hanging out in courtyards, I met some really amazing people with impressive stories. A man from Holland, whom I met in Carrión, had decided that for his fiftieth birthday he would walk to Santiago. There was nothing impressive about that; we were all walking to Santiago. The difference was that he had started at his front door! He had left on March 23 and was to arrive in Santiago on his fiftieth birthday, June 23.

And there was the Japanese woman whom I met about fifteen days outside of Santiago. She had already walked to Santiago from Saint-Jean-Pied-de-Port and was now walking back. I'm sorry, but I could not relate to this. Call me slothful, but for me this is a one-way Camino with no U-turns allowed.

Then there was the woman who was walking with two teenage boys. I found this little arrangement very intriguing. I never got the full story, but apparently the boys were ordered by a court in Italy to go on the Camino, and the woman was a type of social worker. I don't know what they did, but I am sure that the stories I made up in my mind were much more interesting than the truth.

Things I had never thought about or cared about became important to me at the albergues. A good clothesline was a godsend. I hadn't known that there were actually clotheslines anywhere but my Grandma's house, but on the Camino I would get excited on seeing one. My life had become that uncomplicated.

R & R

Terradillos de los Templarios was one of my favorite albergues, and not only because the clotheslines rocked. It also had a great courtyard and small rooms.

We arrived at about 1:00 in the afternoon and were able to check into our room right away. This was always a plus. The room only had four beds, which was wonderful. The showers were plentiful, and the water was hot. I was seeing the Promised Land!

Father Joe and I ended up sharing our room with a really nice couple. We found out only later that the gentleman's snoring sounded like a six-cylinder chain saw. For future planning I made note of his face and the corresponding information.

The courtyard had a great place to wash clothes and plenty of lines on which to hang them. It was a beautiful sunny day, and there was a lot of grass. People were talking, doing laundry and lying in the sun.

Father Joe and I were celebrating the fifteenth anniversary of our Franciscan vows, so we each purchased an ice cream bar and a beer to celebrate. (They really do go together.) We spent the better part of four hours relaxing, reading, praying, napping and reminiscing about the previous fifteen years. It was one of the most enjoyable afternoons of the entire pilgrimage and a day I will never forget. It was almost perfect.

That was, until the robbery. Yes, I was robbed.

My clothes were drying on the super special line provided, and Father Joe and I decided to go have dinner. The albergue did not have a kitchen for pilgrim use, but they offered a wonderful dinner of fish and chips, wine and flan for dessert. Father Joe and I enjoyed the dinner, sharing it with a man from Spain, which was actually a rarity. We met fellow pilgrims from all over the world but few from Spain.

After dinner I went to get my clothes, and it was then I realized I had been robbed. There on the line were my clothes, but the safety pins I had used to secure them were gone. They had been replaced with much cheaper pins. I kid you not!

It was both funny and astonishingly odd. Someone had taken the time to take all my clothes off the line, seize my pins and replace them with their despicable excuse for safety pins. I knew this was the work of more than one person. I imagine whomever the "pin bandits" were must have seen the sparkle of my super grade AAA safety pins, and they simply had to have them. One of the partners in crime must have kept watch on the dining room, and while I was finishing off my flan, the other villain was making off with the loot.

I could only take comfort in the fact that whoever stole my pins needed them more than I.

Community

I think what I enjoyed most about the albergues was the community that developed. This actually took me by surprise, and it was a very beautiful part of my Camino. While we were all very different, coming from various countries and with different religious beliefs, the common experience of the Camino drew us together and created a unique bond. Even to this day, if I meet someone who has walked the Camino, there is a connection between us that is unique.

I have experienced this same communion with men and women who are radically following Christ. There are many common experiences that draw us together. Whether it is the joy we experience in being in relationship with Christ or the freedom that comes from knowing God loves us, a union rests in the depths of our souls.

I have found this to be especially true when it is the cross that binds me with another. When I meet someone who has deeply suffered, there is between us a "knowing" that is beyond words but incredibly real. I suppose this is the most unitive aspect of both the Camino and the Christian life: not simply the walking but the pain that pilgrims bring with them. I may not have known exactly what my fellow pilgrims were going through, but I did know what it was to suffer. And in that we experienced a common bond, a communion, community.

13 : AMAZING GRACE

Being able to celebrate Mass every day is a tremendous privilege. While the Church no longer requires a priest to celebrate Mass daily, it is beyond me why a priest would not want to avail himself of the sacrament each and every day.

Father Joe and I would celebrate Mass daily, with one of us being the main celebrant. During the homily we would often talk about the day, what God was doing in us and what we had experienced over the previous couple of days.

Unfortunately, many of the churches in the little villages were not open, so we celebrated Mass in a few pretty unusual places. A couple times we had Mass in our room in the albergue where we were staying. Once we had Mass on a picnic table on the side of a path, and twice I celebrated next to a small stream, attended by only Father Joe and a couple of ducklings. Other times we would simply wander off the beaten path to find a beautiful place to celebrate.

One day while we were walking, Father Joe and I discussed our most memorable Masses. It was a wonderful time of remembering. I have been amazingly blessed to be able to celebrate Mass in some incredible places.

Always a Priest

Clearly, one of the most memorable was when I was invited, along with my mom and dad, to Pope John Paul II's private chapel to celebrate Mass with him. We were on pilgrimage in Rome for the Jubilee Year when we received the invitation.

The invite stated that we had to be at the Bronze Door at the Vatican by 6:30 AM. We wanted to make sure that we were not late, so we arrived at the beautiful, majestic door at around 5:30. After going through security we were escorted to the Holy Father's office, where I and about a dozen other priests were invited to vest. My parents and the other laypeople waited outside the office before entering the Holy Father's chapel.

Bishop Stanisław Dziwisz, the Holy Father's secretary, entered the office holding some books. He came up to me and the other English-speaking priests and asked in a thick Polish accent if any of us were sinners. I was taken aback by the question, but having never celebrated Mass in the Holy Father's chapel, I was not familiar with protocol. So I raised my hand and stated that, yes, I was a sinner. Sadly, I admitted, I was a big sinner.

The bishop then handed me the books and stated, "Good, you pick songs."

Oh, *singer!*

Needless to say, this broke the nervous tension. One of my brother priests thanked me for a genuine heartfelt confession. I wondered if I would still be allowed to concelebrate Mass.

The Holy Father's private chapel was beautiful—bright and wonderful with lots of light and color. It was more modern than I had expected.

As we entered the chapel, the Holy Father was already praying. I will always remember seeing him kneeling there, kind of slumped over, with strong broad shoulders, dressed in his papal white. I happened to be able to sit right next to him—what a blessing and an honor!

At first I was kind of in awe of the entire situation. For several minutes I sat mere inches from the Holy Father as we prayed and prepared our hearts for the Mass. I could hear him quietly whispering his prayers. This is a memory I will never lose.

As the Holy Father started vesting for Mass, I was struck by something that is very obvious but that had a profound effect on me: The Holy Father is a priest. I know, I know: duh! But for some reason at that point, watching the Holy Father vest for Mass hit me with that reality. His vesting was no different from what I had done thousands of times before. At that moment all nervousness and anxiety left me, and I was able to pray.

Soon the Holy Father began the Mass: "In the name of the Father, and of the Son and of the Holy Sprit." Again, this was exactly what I had done daily for years. I was concelebrating Mass with my brother priest, who happened to be the pope.

As It Is in Heaven

I have celebrated Mass in some of the most amazing churches and basilicas in the world. I also have celebrated at most of the major Marian pilgrimage sites. I celebrated Mass in the tomb of Jesus, in the Church of the Holy Sepulcher in Jerusalem, with only my mother and father and a close friend. I have celebrated in St. Stephen's Cathedral in Vienna, Notre Dame in Paris and St. Peter's in Rome.

I hear people say all the time, "It must be amazing to be able to celebrate Mass at this or that place." I hate to sound as if I am not grateful, because it is wonderful, but it is amazing to say Mass anywhere.

I reflected on this while walking down a dusty trail in the middle of Spain. I had to admit that while all of these opportunities were simply awesome, the reality that God has allowed me even once to take bread and wine and used me to transform them into his Body and Blood far surpasses the magnificence of any "place" that I have been able to celebrate Mass. Whether the Mass is at St. Peter's in Rome with the Holy Father, a picnic table along a path in Spain or around my family's dinner table, it is Jesus who makes himself present and feeds me. In the light of this reality, the "where" is really not that important.

Honestly, once Mass begins I kind of get lost in the "where" and move to the "what." What is taking place here? I am invited into Jesus' eternal sacrifice, an unending celebration with the saints and the angels. I am strengthened with his life. Very quickly the brick and mortar don't matter very much. And frankly neither does the skill of the organist or the talent of the guitarist or the beauty of the statues.

That is not to say these things don't matter, because they do, but in the big picture, the eternal perspective, they shrink in comparison to the grand reality of the Mass: Jesus comes to us in the guise of bread and wine, and our souls are fed. We can never lose sight of this.

Again, good music and preaching are tremendously beneficial. But I find that many people focus on what they think is not right about the liturgy rather than focusing on what is taking place; they focus on what isn't instead of what is.

Jesus *is* making himself present to us and *is* offering his very self to us. I believe if we can focus on this more than on music and preaching and architecture, we will be able to get much more out of the liturgy.

Thank You

The Masses I was able to celebrate on the Camino were very special to me. They were simple—no great music, usually no fabulous cathedral and no huge congregations—but the liturgies were beautiful. It's as if they were stripped down to the most basic essentials: fellowship, the Word, bread and wine, Body and Blood and God's Spirit.

What a gift the Mass is. My heart was filled with gratitude. I wanted to be able to thank God for all that he has done for me, to thank him for the gift of priesthood, the Eucharist, the Camino. However, to simply say "Thank you" seemed inadequate, and "Thank you *very* much" didn't even cover it. Nor did "Thank you *very, very, very* much."

But of course, this is what *Eucharist* means: "thanksgiving." God knew that there would be a day when we were moved to thank him for his goodness to us, and we would feel quite inadequate. He gave us the Eucharist as the most perfect act of thanksgiving. We are able to enter into Jesus' eternal thanksgiving to the Father, and this satisfies; it is enough.

Ultimately it is the Eucharist that feeds us and gives us the strength to continue on the pilgrimage that leads us to the eternal banquet in heaven. What a gift!

14 : DIVINE PROVIDENCE

I was continually amazed at how God took care of things for me. So many times he provided for my every need.

This became particularly evident to me once when I was about two miles outside of Burgos. My left knee started to ache, and within about twenty minutes I could barely walk. I informed Father Joe that I was not sure I could go much farther. We kept walking but very slowly.

After about a half hour, we were within the city limits of Burgos. This is one of the largest cities on the Camino, with hard, hot, concrete streets. We were not sure how far it was to the city center, so we caught a bus, which had us there in a few minutes.

Father Joe and I decided that we wanted to stay close to the cathedral in Burgos, and the albergue was about a thirty-minute walk, so we found a cheap—really cheap—pension. I rested my knee for an hour or two, and by then it felt good enough that I could walk around and enjoy the spectacular cathedral.

But after about an hour of walking, the knee was hurting quite a bit, and I was worried about what I was going to do the next day. I decided that I should probably purchase a knee brace but had no idea where, or if, I could find one. I knew exactly what I wanted, an elastic brace with metal support down the sides of the knee. I prayed that I would be able to find something that would work. How I longed to find a sporting goods store!

All I Needed and More

Father Joe and I decided to sleep in the next morning, a first. I was able to rest pretty well. We got up around 8:00. My knee was sore but not *too* sore, until I walked for a few minutes. It quickly started to ache, and I knew I had to do something. Father Joe and I celebrated Mass and prayed that God would work everything out.

My first stop would be a pharmacy. I figured that some part of my knee must be swollen, and I should be taking more ibuprofen. I arrived at the pharmacy as the front doors were opening—perfect timing. I was somewhat taken aback by the pharmacist, a stunning Spanish woman with long black hair and dark beautiful eyes. But I quickly recovered and asked her, in Spanish, if she spoke *Spanish!* (Perhaps a Spanish lesson would have been a good idea.)

She smiled and stated in perfect English, "Do you mean *English?*"

Yep, that's what I meant.

The pharmacist gave me the ibuprofen and suggested a store that might have a knee brace. We were in luck, because it was only one block away. We departed only to have her come running after me a minute later, waving my walking staff, which I had left at the pharmacy. So I was a little preoccupied.

The store she sent us to did not have what we were looking for, and the clerk suggested a shoe shop about half a block away. But this store would not open for another thirty minutes.

Fortunately, next door was one of the most amazing pastry and coffee shops in this world. There had to be fifty different kinds of pastries filled with creams, chocolates, nuts and fruits. I was like a kid in a candy shop; heck, I *was* a kid in a candy shop. I purchased two extremely large, mouth-watering pastries at about four thousand calories and five hundred grams of fat apiece and ate every bite. I also ordered a cappuccino and then a second. I had had maybe one cup of coffee in the previous ten days, so I savored every sip.

After getting totally jolted on sugar and caffeine, I headed to the shoe shop next door to purchase a brace. The lady at the shop understood English, so I was able to explain precisely what I was looking for. By God's grace she had exactly that.

In the course of the conversation the woman found out I was a priest, and she was very excited that I was walking the Camino. Along with the brace she sold me some pain rub, which was miraculous. She also gave me several prayer cards and asked that I promise to pray for her at the tomb of the apostle in Santiago. I told her I would. And I did.

I was now ready to leave Burgos, and it was not even 11:00 AM. In less than two hours everything simply had fallen into place. God never ceases to amaze me by how he provides for my every need (and in the case of the pastries and coffee, even a few of my wants).

The Sock

In this respect God cannot be outdone.

I was arriving at the small village of Azofra on one of the longest days yet, and I was exhausted. As I was getting my things settled, I noticed that one of my socks had fallen off my backpack, where I had pinned it to dry.

Now, generally a lost sock is not a huge issue. However, on the Camino your socks are some of your most prized possessions. I only had two pairs of socks that I was using for walking, and to lose one sock was a major issue.

I was absolutely exhausted, but I had to go look for the sock. I had no idea when it had fallen off. So with the matching sock in hand, I started backtracking.

I had taken a serendipitous route through the town, so I had to rely on my guardian angel to remind me where I had walked. I walked down small streets by fountains and through alleys, all the way through town, and found nothing. I began to wonder how far I should walk. For all I knew I had lost the sock twelve miles earlier.

As I began to walk the country road leading out of town, I decided I would continue for fifteen more minutes. If I did not find it by then, I would consider it lost. I remember praying. I told God that I was aware that there were far more important things in this world than this silly sock, but I sure would appreciate it if he could arrange for my getting it back.

A few minutes later I noticed three figures on the horizon. As they came closer I could tell they were two adults and a child. Soon I realized they were two elderly women and what I assumed was a granddaughter. The woman on the left was holding something in her hand, and to my sheer and utter delight, it was my long-lost sock. My sock was lost, but now it was found!

I showed the elderly woman the sock in my hand, and I saw one of the purest, most elated smiles—though checkered with missing teeth—I think I have ever seen. Smiling ear to ear and overflowing with joy, she raised her right arm to reveal the matching sock. She seemed more excited than I was. I thanked her profusely, and she kept smiling and patting my cheeks with her weathered hands, saying something over and over again that I didn't understand. But there was no doubt we were communicating.

God takes care of even the little things.

It was a simple thing.

It was a sock.

Thanks, Lord.

15 : EYES ON THE PRIZE

Goals are wonderful things. My long-term goal? I want to go to heaven. Saint Peter says that this is the goal of our faith (see 1 Peter 1:9). But I needed to finish the Camino first. I must admit there were times when I wondered which would come first.

We started walking around 7:00, with our goal for the day Carrión de los Condes, which meant covering about twenty-three miles. By this time on the Camino, I knew my pace well—three miles an hour. So I figured we would reach our destination in about nine hours, with breaks. It was going to be a really long day.

It was one of the coldest days I had encountered since I began the Camino. The previous two days had been cool, but this day was just plain cold. It was cloudy in the morning, which was fairly common, but the clouds did not clear by midmorning as they usually did. In fact the weather got worse. The clouds grew dark and ominous. As of yet I had not experienced really bad weather; I wondered if this might be the day.

Passing through Frómista, I stopped in one of the most beautiful examples of Romanesque architecture in all of Spain. St. Martin's was built in the eleventh century. The symmetry of its reddish-brown brick and rock is beautiful. There are multiple arches in the church, ranging in size from a few feet to nearly twenty feet, and they make the church stunning.

We had already been walking for about three hours, so we took a break. I sat in the ancient church and prayed my Divine Office. I found myself reflecting on the millions of other pilgrims over the centuries who had stopped in this very church in order to offer prayer and seek refuge from storms. There was something wonderful about this church, and I found myself wanting to stay longer, but I knew we had to move on. I prayed that God would take care of the weather and that the storm would not be a problem.

About an hour later the threatening clouds moved past. We were no longer in danger of a major storm. I thanked God and continued walking, keeping my mind fixed on our destination for the day.

We reached Carrión de los Condes around 4:30. Since it was so late in the afternoon, both of the albergues in the small town were full. Eventually we found a hostel that catered to pilgrims. It was a little more expensive than an albergue, nine euros, but we had a five-person room with a private bathroom, so it was definitely worth it.

Carrión de los Condes is a hopping town. I spent about an hour in a local pub enjoying a beer and some peanuts while watching bullfighting on TV with the locals. The cheering and hollering reminded me of Saturday afternoons watching college football with my friends and family.

After the bullfighting Father Joe and I had dinner and headed back to the albergue. It had been a long day, but I was that much closer to Santiago, having reached the goal for the day.

Heaven Bound

I think it unfortunate when people do not set goals for themselves. More often than not they simply float through life without any clear direction.

I find it really sad that many people do not have goals for the things that matter most. Lots of people have goals like making more or saving a certain amount of money. Others have goals such as losing twenty pounds by the class reunion. There is nothing wrong with these goals, but what about goals for the really important things, the things that matter most?

How about setting a goal to be a more patient spouse? One can't just wish to be a more patient spouse and expect it to happen, any more than I could wish to arrive at Santiago and not start walking. There has to be a plan, and there has to be work.

The goal of every Christian ought to be to love more perfectly —and ultimately to get to heaven. I want to be clear: We are not going to just fall into heaven. It is literally harder than hell to get to heaven. It cost Jesus his life to open the gates, and it will cost us the same.

If our goal is heaven, we need to have a plan to see that this happens. I believe our immediate goal should be to live a holy life. What a tragedy if we as Christians don't become holy; holiness is what we have been created for. And to be holy, to grow in our relationship with Christ, we must have a tangible plan.

What do I mean when I say, "Have some kind of plan"? You need to have in place in your life concrete actions that will help you grow in the spiritual life. It is not enough to simply say you want to grow in your relationship with God; you need to be able to articulate how you plan on growing in your relationship with him.

Holiness Essentials

We all need to actively seek conversion. One concrete way that you can do this is by knowing what sin needs to be rooted out of your life. Take a moment and be still. What is the sin that God wants to free you from?

If you can't answer that question, I would encourage you to pray until you can. Sin is simply incompatible with a life of holiness. There is no way we will reach our goal to love more perfectly if we are not continually turning from our sin. My prayer is that you will be able to identify what sin binds you and then work with God's grace in order to root it out.

If you gossip, pray and fast that this sin will be rooted out of your life. In situations where conversation is not edifying, bite your tongue and do not participate. Holiness starts with little steps.

Prayer and participation in the sacraments are essential. You can't simply agree with me: "Yes, I need to pray more; you are right, Father Dave." This is not enough. Look at your schedule, and figure out when you can pray. When can you stop by the local church? On the way home from work or on the way to get groceries?

It is the same with the sacraments. If you would like to go to confession once a month, you need to plan and make it a priority. Or go to Mass on another day in addition to Sunday. It almost never works to do this "when you have time." Life is busy. You need to make the time and do what it takes to follow through.

If you don't have a personal prayer life right now, it is probably not realistic for you to start praying for an hour every day. One does not begin training for a marathon by running twenty miles on the first day. Start small, and grow from there. Being faithful in the small things strengthens you for greater things.

Finally, get help from people who have the same goals as you. I can't imagine walking the Camino without Father Joe. There were moments when one of us was having a difficult time, and the other was there to encourage. Thank God, we don't walk this walk alone. Share with another person your desire to grow in the spiritual life and the steps you are going to take to see that this happens.

There will be times when the road to holiness gets tough. It really is a difficult road, but it is incredibly beautiful—and it is the only way to find the life God has in store for us. God has prepared a place for each of us in heaven. May each of us receive all the grace we need to stay on the path and to keep walking.

16 : SICK AS A DOG

Either Father Joe or I really should have learned more Spanish before we went to Spain. The pharmacy incident was not the only awkward moment.

One time Father Joe and I were in a park, and a young Spanish boy interrupted our relaxation. I could not understand what he was yelling, so I yelled back, in Spanish, that I did not speak Spanish.

This, of course, was absolutely correct. God has gifted me with some things; a facility for languages is not one of them.

The boy yelled louder, so I responded in kind. He yelled louder; I yelled louder. Soon he came up to us, and we discovered that he wanted a match to light his cigarette. We did not have one, so he left us alone.

Father Joe was kind of laughing, and I asked him what was so funny. He stated that I had yelled at the boy that *he* didn't speak Spanish. The boy would yell, "I speak Spanish," to which I would reply, "You don't speak Spanish."

Of course, what I meant to say was that *I* didn't speak Spanish—that darn tower of Babel. At least this mistake did not cost us any money.

Luxury and Sacrifice

When Father Joe and I arrived in Hermanillos, all of the albergues were full, so we split up to look around and see what else might be available. There were at least two hotels and a pension or two in the small village. Both of the places I went to were full, but Father Joe came back excited. He stated that a room in the hotel was only fourteen euros, and it looked really nice.

Only in Burgos had we paid that much for lodging, but we really didn't have a lot of choices, so we headed to the hotel. On checking in we slapped down fourteen euros and waited for our key. The woman looked at us with a confused glare.

I thought the place looked a little nicer than a fourteen-euro joint. It then occurred to me that perhaps it was fourteen euros per person. Father Joe and I asked, but we were not able to communicate very well, so we slapped down another fourteen euros. She then wrote down on a piece of paper "40."

I see. Fourteen euros apiece would have been a steal.

Well, we didn't have a lot of options, so we each coughed up six more euros and headed to our room. Hmmm, our room, our private quiet room, with a private bathroom and a shower with hot water and lots of it. That was the best twenty euros I have ever spent in my life!

Dinner was once again fascinating. I had heard a lot of different stories about why people were walking the Camino, but here was a topper. The gentleman with whom I had dinner was walking the Camino in order to check out places for fly-fishing. He was writing an article for a magazine about the opportunities for fly-fishing in Spain, specifically on the Camino route. He shared that he was actually frustrated because there were not as many streams as he had hoped for.

Tough luck. Being a pilgrim can be sacrificial. As it would happen, fish was the main course for the pilgrims' meal that night, and we enjoyed talking about fly-fishing and our Camino.

The next day's walk to Mansilla de la Sierra looked like a brief fifteen-mile trek. I knew that it was going to be totally flat, and my body felt really good, so I was expecting a pretty easy walk. We departed around 7:00 on a gorgeous day. It was slightly cool, perfect walking weather, though as the sun rose over the horizon, it became evident that it was going to be a little warmer than previous days.

As was expected, the path was straight and flat. But oddly, about two hours into the walk, I became worn out, really drained. I felt as if I had been walking all day.

As the miles went by, I began to think something was wrong. Perhaps it was because it was hotter and my body wasn't used to the heat. I had learned that dinner the night before is the most important factor toward how I was going to feel the next day, but I had had a great dinner the night before. I had drunk plenty of water, so I didn't think I was dehydrated.

At around 10:30 in the morning, I *knew* there was something wrong with me. We had walked at a pretty good pace, so we were only about forty-five minutes from Mansilla. I could not wait to get there so that I could sit down.

Insult to Injury

When we arrived at the albergue, we discovered that it did not open till 1:00 PM. In cases like this, pilgrims place their backpacks next to the wall outside the albergue in the order in which they arrived. They then go and explore the town or get something to eat, returning a few minutes before the albergue opens to retrieve their packs and their place in line.

Father Joe and I placed our packs in the line. I sat down and told him that I was exhausted. He decided to walk around a little and look at the town.

After sitting for a few minutes, I realized I was going to be sick. I entered the albergue, and quickly they told me, "Not open." I explained that I needed the bathroom because I was sick. They did not understand. I used the little Spanish I knew, "*enfermo!*" and rubbed my stomach. They got the point and took me to the bathroom. I proceeded to get sick about every fifteen to thirty minutes for the next six hours.

The cleaning staff called Maria, the host of the albergue. Maria was a really sweet woman who spoke English quite well. She showed me to the room across from the bathroom, which was a private room with four beds for those who were ill. It was the first albergue that I had been in that had a special room for someone not feeling well.

Maria asked me a few questions, and it seemed as if she might be a nurse. I asked her if she was, and she stated no, she was a veterinarian. That was perfect for me, because I was sick as a dog. Maria took my temperature, and it was around 102°F. She stated, "You really *are* sick."

Um, yeah.

Maria said she would call a doctor and see what he thought. She returned a short time later and said that the doctor wanted to wait for an hour or so to see if rest and hydration would help me feel better. However, hydration was difficult due to the fact that I was not able to keep anything down. This was not a great day.

Now, as if this was not difficult enough, I had a problem on my right heel. For the previous few days I had felt a blister forming. It wasn't a normal blister that you could see. It was on the back edge of my heel, in the "tough" part of the foot. So when I was lying on my back in bed, I could not put my heel on the bed. I tried to poke the blister with a needle in order to drain it, but I kept getting sick, so I was not successful.

Father Joe returned, and I was frustrated and asked him if he could help me. It was quite a scene. I lay over the edge of my bed, on my stomach with a bucket on the floor in front of me. Father Joe was at the end of the bed with a needle poking around in my foot. "I can't really see it. There, is that it? How about that? Oh, now I see it. Hmmm. Is that better?"

I felt like a pincushion. But eventually Father Joe was able to fix my heel so that I could rest it on the bed without discomfort. What relief!

Rejoice in the Measure

"All this for the King. All this for the King. All this for the King..."

As I was lying in bed, I recalled what I had written in my journal the night before in my plush hotel. It was about sharing in the sufferings of Christ. I had felt that I was not doing that very well. I had written, "Jesus, I accept whatever comes and pray that I may rejoice in the ways that I may share in your suffering (see 1 Peter 4:13). May I be given the grace to share in your suffering with joy."

I know, I know, what was I thinking? Father Joe stated that he would like to edit my journal each evening in order to delete unnecessary passages. But this grace really was what I wanted.

So there I was lying on my bed praying. I asked God if this really was what he had for me. I then heard him clearly say to me, "Yes."

Wow, I hadn't seen that coming. In that moment I had complete confidence that my being sick really was part of what God had for me. He gave me the tremendous grace of acceptance.

The only way I can really explain what was going on was that my experience was holy. I know that may sound crazy, but lying on the bed, sick with a fever, nauseated, with my body aching, had become sacred. There was an intense communion with God that I will never forget. It was one of the more profound experiences of my Camino.

I know that accepting suffering is a place where I need greater transformation. So often when I am hurting, I bear it all by myself. This is tragic because it does not have to be that way.

First, I always have the option of uniting my sufferings with those of Christ. To the degree that I am able to do this, my suffering can actually help make me holy. My suffering is not meaningless.

A friend of mine was experiencing great suffering and was somewhat frustrated with God. While praying one day she heard God say, "When are you going to make pain your companion instead of your enemy?" She went on to consider the fact that a companion goes somewhere with you, even accompanies you on a journey. If we allow suffering to be our companion, it will ultimately lead us home to the Father.

I have found myself thinking and praying about that often. Suffering is not something we need to escape from or walk away from; rather we can embrace it. When we are able to do that, we find Jesus showering us with his love from the cross. Amazing.

We also can offer our suffering for others, and there is a tremendous splendor in this. Be it a family member who is sick or has wandered away from God or a coworker in the middle of a divorce, we can offer our pain and suffering for someone. Only in heaven will we fully know the benefit the individual received, but even now we can have peace knowing that our suffering is not in vain.

How amazing it is that the living God knows what it is to suffer. He knows our pain and sorrow, our loneliness and fears. God did not simply send us a word of comfort; rather he sent his Son to show us how to suffer and to meet us in the middle of our pain. I do not suffer alone, and my pain is not useless. It can show me Jesus' face and reveal his love in a way that cannot be found any other way.

Reflecting on these realities was a cause of tremendous grace and peace. I was still sick and throwing up, but I was peaceful.

Early in the evening Maria returned to my room with some medicine. She said that the doctor had instructed her to give it to me, and she thought it might break my fever and help me feel better. To this day I don't know what she gave me, but it was remarkable. Within thirty minutes my fever was gone, and I did not get sick again. Some might wonder why I was not given the medication four hours earlier, but I knew why—thank you, Lord.

Later in the evening Father Joe and I celebrated Mass in our room. While I felt a lot better, I was pretty whipped, so I remained in bed. It was a beautiful Mass. I love the simplicity and familiarity of the faith. There in a small, dimly lit room, we listened to the Word, we took bread and wine, we remembered and prayed the words of consecration, which are so comforting and life giving, and we received Jesus. I rejoiced in God's presence in my life and was so grateful to be on pilgrimage to Santiago.

17 : LEAD ME

I can't remember for sure the first time I saw the cute elderly couple. It was hard to tell exactly how old they were, but clearly they were significantly older than most of the other pilgrims. The *Brazil* sweatshirt and hat gave me a clue that perhaps they were from Brazil. (I have a keen sense for the obvious.)

I remember seeing them in a type of open-air market, and they were looking at the fruit, the varied colors of which reminded me of the big sixty-four-color box of crayons I had as a boy. The wife would take a piece of fruit and hand it to her husband, who would bring it close to his face and smell it. They looked as if they had followed this routine for years.

The next time I saw them I was sick in bed. No need to go into that particular event again, but the elderly couple shared the infirm room with me. Neither was ill, but I think Maria allowed them to stay in the room because of their age. I learned that they were in fact from Brazil and that Anthony was sixty-nine and Teresa was sixty-eight. They had decided that it would be good to walk the Camino one more time. Yes, one more time.

Anthony was a retired doctor, and he had an innate ability to discern a given situation. After asking me a few questions, he figured I probably had eaten something bad or had some kind of virus. There was a gentleness and a genuine concern about him that was beautiful. I imagined that his patients had loved him.

When Anthony found out that I was a priest, he was excited. He informed me that he and his wife would do anything I needed. "Even if it is 3:00 in the morning and you want some water, let us know. We will get you anything you need. It is really an honor for us to be sharing a room with you." I suspect the same offer would have been extended to anyone, regardless of their being a priest or not.

I was already kind of emotional, given the fact that I was awfully sick and extremely uncomfortable, but their offer of kindness and the sincerity with which it was presented were extremely touching. With tears in my eyes, I said I would let them know.

What an amazing couple they were. I really couldn't imagine walking the Camino in my late sixties, and they were doing it for the second time. Incredible.

Charity Prevailing

Oh, and did I mention that Anthony was blind? He explained to me that he was not *totally* blind—he could see some lights and darks—and that he had only been like this for a few years. I can't recall exactly what caused his loss of sight. It now made sense to me why he had held the fruit so close to his face in the market: Not only was he smelling it, but he was also trying to look at it.

Even now as I reflect back on my time with this couple, I am touched by the charity that they exuded. There was something very different and exceptional about them. I think it must have been what Jesus saw in Nathaniel, whom he stated had "no guile" (John 1:47). There was a radiance, a goodness about Anthony and Teresa that was potent.

I saw them two or three times the next day, and what a moving sight they were. Teresa would stand in front of Anthony, he would place his left hand on her right shoulder, and they would set out. They moved more slowly than most of the other pilgrims, but they were walking. Teresa explained that cities were the most difficult for them. "Too many streets and crowds; we really prefer the paths through the countryside."

What an inspiration they were.

Due to my being sick, the manager of the albergue arranged a ride for me to the next town, León, which was only about a twelve-minute ride. I wrestled for a few minutes with accepting the ride. "I want to walk," I weakly demanded. However, I knew that it was a good idea to accept the offer. I could not afford to lose a day, as I really wanted to be at the cathedral in León for Pentecost. Also, one of the golden rules of a pilgrim is to accept whatever God sends you, and that day he sent me a ride to León.

The Benedictine Sisters operated the albergue in León, and they did things a little differently there than at the other albergues. Men were on the second floor to the right of the main entrance, and women were on the left. No one was allowed in the other sex's section. Some of the pilgrims seemed a little put off by the "senseless restrictions," but most took it in stride. It was all part of the experience of the Camino.

In the evening Father Joe and I prayed with the sisters, and we found it beautiful to join a community for prayer. They had created prayer sheets for the pilgrims and made everyone feel welcome. The sisters looked beautiful in their habits, scattered throughout the ancient choir stalls. I would guess there were about twenty sisters, with a few younger women who appeared to be novices.

The eldest sister sat on the right side of the church, where she could see the pilgrims entering from the opposite side. Each and every pilgrim was greeted with a glowing smile. I wondered how many pilgrims over the decades this loving, aged nun had received. What a wonderfully simple and touching ministry she had: smiling at pilgrims.

All Is Gift

The cathedral in León is exquisite. It is a late thirteenth-century Gothic cathedral, with narrow pointed arches and ordered straight lines. The stone walls keep the church relatively cool, even though it was getting warm outside. Clearly the Gothic design of the church raises one's spirit to God. If a medieval cathedral is supposed to be able to educate the visitor in the faith, what a magnificent instructor this church is.

To the right as you enter the cathedral is the statue *Santiago Peregrino*, Saint James, which is well worn due to the millions of pilgrims touching him as they seek the saint's intercession. There were over 125 mammoth stained-glass windows, and they were exquisite. What a joy it was to stand in the middle of this towering cathedral and be showered by a rainbow of light emanating from the windows. It seemed a very appropriate house for God.

As I was exiting the cathedral after the Pentecost Mass, I ran into Anthony and Teresa one last time. Teresa was standing in front of the cathedral describing it to her husband. This beautiful scene is stamped in my memory.

I approached them to say hi and to let them know I was feeling better. They were happy that my sickness did not delay my walk. We parted ways, promising to keep each other in our prayers. I knew they would be people I would continue to reflect on and think about. I had no doubt that God was going to use them again to teach me.

While in León I did something I had not previously done, nor would I do again. The sisters at the albergue would wash your clothes for you. I don't recall the price, but I think it was a few euros. Reasoning that I was helping the sisters, I dropped off all my clothes before I went out for the afternoon—anything to help the sisters.

Father Joe and I relaxed in a park for a couple of hours and then caught dinner at a little café. Not being totally sure how my stomach would react, I had a simple rice and chicken dish that was delicious. My stomach seemed settled, and I was glad to be able to eat again.

I spent some time in the sisters' chapel before bed, and I was overwhelmed by God's goodness. Twenty-four hours earlier I had been running a high fever and could not keep down the smallest sip of water. In the midst of it all God was present to me. He was present in my sickness, in Anthony and Teresa, in the Benedictine Sisters and in the beauty of the cathedral. And he was present in my "surrender" to accept a ride to León.

It had been a crazy two days. I was still a bit weak, but all in all I felt ready to go. And I had been given a gift to be able to see God in many circumstances.

I went to bed that night filled with Christ's peace, knowing that he continued to walk with me and that he was guiding me. I slept well that night.

18 : GROWING STRONG

There were a number of significant milestones along the Camino. I remember early on seeing painted on a rusty drainage pipe, "Santiago 687 km," and thinking I would never get there. I recall clearly the "500 km" sign, oddly being relieved that I only had five hundred kilometers left. Halfway was a major milestone and cause for great rejoicing. I stopped to pose for a picture when we reached the "150 km" sign. Goodness, I was basically done!

One thing that was actually kind of frustrating was that, beginning at around 150 kilometers (about ninety miles), there was a marker every half kilometer. I honestly did not like those markers, because they reminded me how slow the pace was. My body had adjusted very well, and I was honestly enjoying the walk each day. My, how far I had come.

While at the beginning of the Camino I was nervous about getting lost, this proved to be a useless concern. The *flechas amarillas* proved to be very reliable in keeping us pointed in the right direction. However, one day it occurred to me that a mischievous twelve-year-old and a can of yellow spray paint could make a pilgrim's life miserable.

We arrived at Sarria, which is 117 kilometers from Santiago. In order to receive the *Compostela*, a pilgrim has to walk at least a hundred kilometers, so Sarria is a very popular starting place. I have to admit that I felt that starting in Sarria was somewhat of a "pilgrimage light," but people do what they are able. In Sarria there were many new faces.

The town has several albergues, and most of the people in mine were just beginning their pilgrimage. They were excited, fresh and ready to go. All of their supplies were shiny and new, and they were still figuring out how everything worked. There was a spring in their step that would soon be lost as they began walking. Oh yes, they were oh so clueless, with no idea what they were getting into. But for now they couldn't wait to begin their walk.

Some of the newbies appeared to be watching me out of the corner of their eye. I felt like a senior in high school being watched by the new freshmen. It was evident that I knew the ropes and the little ones were going to watch and learn.

It was fun to see these new pilgrims and reminisce about my own beginning three weeks back. It seemed like both an eternity and just moments ago that I had been in their shoes: getting things settled to begin my walk the following day. But I was 440 miles into a 500-mile walk. I was close to finishing; they were just beginning.

Rather quickly I was struck with differing perspectives. I heard one of the rookie pilgrims talking about how far they had to walk, "over a hundred kilometers." At the same time I could not believe how little I had to walk, "only a hundred more." It's all in one's perspective.

The next morning lightning and thunder woke us. Welcome to the Camino, my freshmen friends! Many of them slapped on their gear and trudged out into the rain.

This was the first time over the entire Camino that Father Joe and I had encountered hard rain, and we were not sure how to proceed. We decided to wait a bit to see if it would blow over. Given that the day's walk was not that far, fourteen miles, we had some time to spare. We had a more leisurely breakfast than usual, eating some rice pudding-type stuff that I had discovered at a store a few days earlier. It was cheap and tasted pretty good.

By about 7:45 AM it looked as if the rain was mostly over, so we began walking.

Not Fair!

Very soon a disturbing feeling came over me. I thought about the fact that the people who started walking in Sarria would get the same *Compostela* that I did. It just didn't seem right. I was going to walk five hundred miles, they were only going to walk sixty, and we would both get the same "prize." Obviously I should get something more or bigger. I did more work and should be rewarded accordingly.

It reminded me of my little nephew's reaction to his eight-year-old cousin's being baptized and receiving his First Communion all on the same day. "What a rip-off! I have been Catholic all my life (six years), and I don't get to go to Communion. He is only Catholic for one day, and he gets to go."

This in turn reminded me of the Bible story in which an employee is frustrated that a fellow employee gets paid the same wage for less work. The master replies, "Friend, I am doing you no wrong; did you not agree with me for a denarius? Take what belongs to you and go; I choose to give to this last one as I give to you. Am I not allowed to do what I choose with what belongs to me? Or do you begrudge my generosity?" (Matthew 20:13-15).

By God's grace I quickly found myself repenting. I wasn't doing the Camino to get a *Compostela*. I was doing it because I wanted to give myself to God. I wanted to thank him for allowing me to be a priest. How easily I get distracted.

I was bothered by the fact that my initial desire had been to give myself to the Lord and offer him a sacrifice of love, and in a brief moment outside of Sarria my Camino had become about what I was getting out of it. As I thought more about this, I realized that I do this a lot. I start something with good intentions, but somewhere along the way I get confused.

I think a lot of people do this. A man marries his bride and desires to fully give himself to her, but all too quickly he gets frustrated because he feels he is not receiving as much as he is giving. An individual volunteers at the parish and then gets angry that no one else is volunteering. Or people go to pray or attend Mass to *give* God glory and adoration and get frustrated that they don't *get* anything out of it. How fickle is the human heart.

At that moment I recommitted myself to the Lord and reminded myself that it is more blessed to give than to receive. I reminded myself that all I ever wanted was to give God thanks.

My Blessing

The more I thought about the people who started walking in Sarria, the more I actually felt sorry for them. They really weren't lucky, as I had originally thought. There is so much they were going to miss out on because they only were walking for five or six days.

First off, their entire pilgrimage was going to be difficult. I recalled my first days: My body hurt, and my feet were killing me. Had I only walked five days, my experience of the Camino would have been miserable, in that I wouldn't have been able to work through the pain and realize that I was not going to hurt all the time.

I may have missed the experience of finding the pain strangely beautiful. I would not have had the experience of walking all day and being extremely tired at the end but also feeling exceptionally strong. I never would have had the experience of growing, developing and honestly becoming stronger.

It really was a beautiful experience for me to work through the pain and discomfort and continue to go forward. On a very human level, I had a tremendous sense of accomplishment. But much deeper than that, I was pulled on by a desire to be more conformed to the person of Christ, and I knew that my continuing to walk would help bring this about. By continuing to walk I was invited to a greater trust in God and the realization that my next step would be met by a God who was for me and was ever calling me closer to his heart. As I walked I rejoiced at what I saw God doing in my heart.

My day ended at Portomarín at about 12:45 PM. With the exception of a few brief minutes of light rain, during which I found shelter in a small barn, I stayed dry the entire day.

Portomarín was one of the most beautiful towns on the Camino. My albergue was perched on a niche in a hill overlooking an extremely large, stunning, crystal-blue lake. The setting was simply gorgeous. Father Joe and I, joined by a young German girl, ate dinner on a porch overlooking the lake.

Andrea was in her early twenties and was Catholic. As soon as she learned we were priests, she was super excited. Each morning she would ask when and where we were going to have Mass and if it would be OK if she joined us, which I believe she did almost every day for the rest of the Camino.

After a fantastic dinner of pasta, salad, chicken, fries and, of course, wine, I had to look for soap. The bar I had used for the entire Camino had become small enough to be basically useless. Portomarín had a few small stores, and I was able to find what I needed with great ease.

Upon arriving back at the albergue, I grabbed a beer and joined a large group of men from all over Europe who were watching a World Cup soccer match. I thoroughly enjoyed the camaraderie that develops between men when they're having a beer and watching an athletic event. For a brief hour there were no language barriers. What a great evening.

I went to bed that night unbelievably joyful and content. It had been a wonderful day.

19 : NEARING THE END

We arrived at our destination at about 2:30 PM, having done a sixteen-mile walk. As we came closer to the finish of the Camino, we found ourselves taking more breaks. At around 11:00 AM we had stopped for a big lunch with a couple from Australia. I could count on one hand the number of times we had stopped for a sit-down lunch at a café, but since Robert and Jenny invited Father Joe and me, and we took them up on their offer.

We were in a small no-name town, and lunch was some kind of omelet dish with potatoes. We sat at our table for well over an hour, talking and watching other pilgrims go storming by us. They seemed to be in a hurry to get to the next destination, which we figured would be there no matter how slowly or quickly we walked. Slow down, enjoy life—or at least lunch.

But as great as the lunch was, it was clearly not the highlight of the day. No, the day's highlight was most certainly my *running with the bulls*. God must have known that I desired to run with the bulls in Pamplona, so he arranged this little encounter.

I was walking through a tiny village with no more than a half dozen houses. Suddenly, out of the corner of my eye, I saw them stampeding. What a sight, probably eight to ten of the biggest, darkest, meanest bulls I had ever laid eyes on. These beasts were moving in my direction, and one of us was going to have to give way. I was determined that it was not going to be me.

OK, absolute truth be told, stampeding may be a stretch for what the bulls were actually doing, but they were certainly moving in my direction. Or at least it looked as if they were.

I had to act quickly. I grabbed my camera, ran over to Father Joe, gave him the camera, showed him exactly how to use it, changed the batteries, put in a new disk and rushed back to the path of the bulls. I crept in front of one of them, and Father Joe snapped a picture of me running with the bull right behind.

Except that the bull wasn't actually running at the time. Nor was he a him, I would later find out. But it was an exhilarating experience nonetheless.

As I was walking away from this harrowing encounter, I admitted to myself that I had great respect for the way the animals stood up to me. But I would have to say that I was most impressed with the elderly, hunchbacked lady who was corralling them. What a woman!

A significant revelation came to me as I was walking that morning. I realized that we were about forty-five miles from Santiago. First off, it was cool being so close. But it hit me, when I started walking at 7:30, that if I were to take a car to Santiago, I could be having breakfast in some little café in Santiago by 8:30 AM. I was a forty-minute drive from Santiago, but I was still a three-day walk from there.

In reflecting on being close to the finish, I also considered the fact that I really couldn't do anything differently. I had to get up in the morning, pack my things, start walking till I got to my destination and then go through the end-of-the-day ritual. The journey is what it is and will be complete in its due time. Perseverance is a good thing.

I am sure that my running with the bulls or, to be more precise, walking with the cows caused me to reflect on my mortality. Or maybe it was my getting closer to the end that caused me to reflect on final things. Anyway, I don't know when my journey to God is finally going to end, and honestly, I wouldn't want to know. I need to live this life the same each day. I need to get up in the morning and try to run the race to the best of my ability.

Each day I should desire to love better, be a better priest, be holier and more faithful. What is demanded of me is not significantly different, whether I am just beginning my walk or nearing the end.

What I desire most is to be faithful and to finish the race. It doesn't matter if I finish running or crawling; all I want is to finish and to hear the Father say to me, "Well done, good and faithful servant" (Matthew 25:23).

I can't give up; I must keep going.

20 : THE FINAL DAYS

The last days of the Camino were fantastic. I can't believe I just said that, but they really were.

On one of the last days, we arrived at Ribadiso, which is a pretty town with an emerald green stream running through it. This was the scheduled stop, but Father Joe and I were both feeling really good, so we decided we would keep walking. There was no real reason other than that we could.

The next town was Arzúa, which was only a little over two miles away. We had a hard time finding an albergue there, and we ended up staying in one that had only been open for about a week. It was a fancy place, costing about nine euros, which was more than most places we had stayed. We threw caution to the wind and splurged.

After getting settled we went looking for a place for dinner. We ended up at a little café that was advertising "American" hamburgers, which sounded good to me. I will take their word that what was served really was hamburger, but after dinner I realized that I missed home.

These final days were filled with excitement and anticipation. I had resisted thinking about the finish for two main reasons. One, I did not want to miss what was going on at the time. Sometimes we can focus on the past and the future so much that we miss special things that are going on around us.

The second reason was that if I had thought about the end at the beginning, I would have been depressed because there was so much to do and so far to go. It would have been overwhelming. But in just two days I was going to be finished with my Camino, so now I could get excited.

Father Joe and I did a novena for the last nine days, praying that we would finish well and not miss any of the grace that God had for us. I truly felt I was ready to complete my Camino and was in a good place. The exhilaration of being finished was getting stronger and stronger each day and with every step. It wasn't in just me; you could sense it in all of the other pilgrims. Dinners lasted longer, more breaks were taken, countless stories were told, and wine was enjoyed. Laughter filled the air.

We spent our last night before arriving at Santiago in Arca do Pino. It had been a short day of about fourteen miles, and we arrived at the albergue at around 11:00 AM. Since it was so early, Father Joe and I briefly discussed going on to Santiago: It was only thirteen miles away, and we could be there by midafternoon. However, we decided that there was no reason to get there early, and we should just as well enjoy the rest of the day relaxing.

The albergue did not open till 1:00, so Father Joe and I left our backpacks in line and went for a walk through the town. It was a magnificent day. We stopped at a local pub for a long lunch and watched World Cup Soccer with the locals. We sat in a park and enjoyed the tranquility of the moment. We laughed and reminded each other of funny things that had happened over the last thirty days.

We experienced much joy, anticipation and excitement. It reminded me of the feeling I had before graduations, with everyone energized and expectant. It made waiting for Santa seem dull.

As I suppose was fitting, it turned out that the last albergue was probably the worst of the entire Camino. The bathrooms and showers were out of control, with no sense of privacy. There was mold on the walls and on the ceiling of our room, and I was on the top bunk, with my face only inches from the ceiling. It was disgusting, and I loved it. It was the last night, and nothing was going to bother me.

Finishing Strong

The final day we began walking a little earlier than other days, leaving around 6:00. We wanted to be sure we were in Santiago for the Pilgrims' Mass at noon. The concluding walk was only thirteen miles, so I knew that with leaving early we would have plenty of time.

About eight miles into the walk, we arrived at San Marcos, which is situated on a hill overlooking the city of Santiago. There is a large cross and a monument depicting pilgrims on their way to Santiago. Among the most famous was Pope John Paul II, who visited in 1982 and again in 1989 for World Youth Day.

I was excited to get to San Marcos, because I had been told that we could actually see the Cathedral of St. James from the crest of the hill. It was partially cloudy, so I couldn't see it, but that didn't bother me. I knew the cathedral was there, and in about an hour I would be in it.

Soon after San Marcos I stopped and looked in awe at the "Santiago" sign that revealed we were entering the town. I can imagine that only seeing the "Heaven" sign will cause me more excitement. I am sure my smile and the joy in my heart could have lit the town.

It wasn't just being done walking that thrilled me, as nice as that was; it was the completion of everything that had gone into this pilgrimage: the planning and the prayer, the pain and the joy, as well as the thank-you to God for allowing me to be a priest. It was all too much—sheer exhilaration.

However, it was still a good walk to the cathedral. As was always the case, following the *flechas amarillas* (how I had grown to love those little things) was difficult in the city. The many other signs and markings made it hard to follow the path. It was taking us a while, and Father Joe was getting a little concerned that we might have gone the wrong way. He turned around and said to me, "We should be there by now."

At that very moment I saw the Cathedral of St. James over Father Joe's right shoulder. "Joe, turn around. Look, there it is."

We could only see the steeple, and we were still several blocks away. But we were elated. I felt tears welling up inside me.

The next few blocks were a blur, and I am quite certain I was walking on air. I approached the cathedral from the back right side. I walked down a narrow street into an archway, where a street musician was playing some corny '80s love song. I then turned left into the large cobblestone plaza in front of the burial place of Saint James. I was home.

It was a very personal time, and Father Joe and I did not speak to each other. The other pilgrims, too, were silent. The first moments before the cathedral were unbelievably private and had to be experienced alone. Maybe it was the culmination of two years of planning, thinking and praying, or maybe it was relief that five hundred miles of walking were mercifully finished. Perhaps it was thinking of the millions of pilgrims over eleven hundred years who had stood in the exact place I was standing with an overwhelming sense of gratitude. Possibly it was remembering those whose enduring wish was to pray at the saint's tomb but who for one reason or another were not able to finish, some giving their very lives in the process.

At any rate, there weren't hugs and high fives; those would come later.

Giving Thanks

I walked to the middle of the plaza and faced the cathedral. And at 10:15 AM, on the vigil of the Solemnity of the Body and Blood of Christ, I took off my backpack and knelt down. I looked up at the most beautiful church I had ever seen and was silent, really silent. I was amazed by grace. There, kneeling on the reddish-gray cobblestones, I prayed. The prayer of my heart was what it had always been.

> Thank you.
> Thank you for allowing me to be a priest.
> Thank you for loving me.
> Thank you for forgiving me.
> Thank you for living for me.
> Thank you for dying for me.
> Thank you for the cross.
> Thank you for the suffering.
> Thank you for saving me.
> Thank you for rescuing me.
> Thank you for baptism.
> Thank you for the Eucharist.
> Thank you for my Franciscan life.
> Thank you for family and friends.
> Thank you for letting me walk the Camino.

Jesus, I have done all this for you, my King.
Thank you.

I honestly don't have any idea how long I was there, but once I was finished the celebration began. Father Joe and I gave each other hugs and high fives and stood and stared at the cathedral. We had a great sense of satisfaction and relief. But we really didn't say much; we just looked.

Finally I asked, "Shall we?"

"Let's."

So Father Joe and I marched up two flights of stairs to the entrance of the Cathedral of St. James in Santiago, Spain.

There is a prescribed ritual one follows when concluding the Camino, but we decided that we did not want to be rushed and would do it later. So we spent only a few minutes in the cathedral offering thanks. We wanted to find a place to stay and stash our backpacks before the noon Mass.

Many of the rooms in the pensions were already booked, so we had to wander around a bit, but eventually we found a wonderful little place about two blocks from the cathedral. The room still needed to be cleaned, but the owner, a lovely, grandmotherly, Spanish lady, invited us to go ahead and leave our backpacks. We were glad to accept her invitation.

Holy Smoke

By this time it was about 11:30, so Father Joe and I quickly went to the cathedral. We wanted to make sure we would be able to concelebrate, and we were not sure how that would be arranged.

As it turned out the cathedral staff was very accustomed to having concelebrating priests. There were about ten priests in all, but they had not walked the Camino. They were simply visiting the cathedral as a pilgrimage site. It was lots of fun talking with them about our experiences. I sensed their looking at me with a keen sense of respect: "He walked the Camino."

The Mass was beautiful. While it was predominantly in Spanish, the readings were done in a couple different languages, as were the Prayers of the Faithful. It was wonderful to look out into the congregation and see people with whom I had spent one of the most amazing months of my life. Everyone was beaming.

One of the parts of this Mass that I was greatly looking forward to was the incensation with the famous giant thurible—you know, that thing they put incense in at Mass. The thurible in Santiago is about four feet tall and weighs over a hundred pounds. It swings from the ceiling of the cathedral. The story is that in days of old, the church would be so full of smelly pilgrims that it was necessary to have a large thurible loaded with incense in order to counter the stench.

With the help of nine men, the thurible is attached to a rope that has been lowered through a pulley system attached to the ceiling far above the main altar. At the appropriate time each of the concelebrating priests is allowed to place incense in the thurible; this was a thrill. In most parishes this placement is done with a dainty silver baby spoon, but not in Santiago. The incense is in a large silver bucket, and the "spoon" is more like a small garden shovel. It was a really cool experience.

The thurible is then raised with ropes, and the men begin to swing it. In a matter of seconds the thurible was catapulting far above the pilgrims from the left to the right transept and back again. Incense was filling the cathedral, and you could literally see fire in it as it swung from the ceiling like a huge pendulum.

Had pilgrims not been kept at bay with a rope, someone could have been hit. There is little doubt that a blow from this thurible could have caused serious injury or even death—I am not exaggerating!

The incensation only took a few minutes, but it was an unbelievably memorable experience.

The Pilgrim Ritual

At the conclusion of Mass it was time to perform the prescribed ritual of the pilgrim's entrance into the cathedral. This involved first placing one's hand on the Tree of Jesse, which is a spectacular marble column created by the artist Mateo in the twelfth century. Many of the most significant characters of the Bible are etched in it. These persons have waited patiently over the centuries to greet arriving pilgrims.

The column depicts Christ, who reigns in his glory, surrounded by his apostles, with Saint James beneath Jesus and the pilgrims below Saint James. The column is worn by years of pilgrims venerating it, so the five indentations for one's fingers are a permanent part of the column.

I walked around the column, and there sits a statue of Mateo himself. As the ritual prescribes, I placed my head to his, seeking his intercession and the same grace and inspiration he received when he created the magnificent column.

Finally I walked down the right side of the cathedral and just past the main altar, then turned left to climb a small flight of stairs. Standing behind and above the main altar, I embraced a large silver statue of Saint James. I had only a brief moment to rest my head on his broad shoulder to thank him for his prayers; I had to allow the countless other pilgrims the same honor.

While this ritual took only a few minutes, it was an important part of completing my Camino. It was the exact same practice that millions of pilgrims had done before, and at that moment I felt particularly close to each one of them. I doubted that I fully understood what I had just completed.

The last detail that had to be taken care of was visiting the pilgrims' office in order to obtain my *Compostela*. While I had determined on several occasions that I was not walking the Camino simply to get the *Compostela*, there also was no way I was going to forgo it.

The office was located about half a block from the cathedral, on the second floor of a very nondescript building. There were not many other pilgrims in line, so we waited only a few minutes. When it was my turn, I handed in my credentials, which were filled with colorful stamps from thirty-one days of walking. The lady behind the desk looked at the credentials and asked me the purpose of my Camino, religious or secular. I stated it was religious. She then asked me if I had actually walked. I stated that I had. Apparently she believed me, and she wrote my name, in Latin, on my *Compostela* and handed it to me. "Congratulations."

That was it. I was done. No great ceremony. No ringing bells or trumpet blasts. With a simple handing of an eight-by-ten certificate, I had finished my Camino.

Or had I?

21 : IT IS FINISHED

For the last few days of the Camino, I felt a yearning in my heart that I could not explain. It was a tugging deep within me that was always present but vaguely outside of me. I felt I was being drawn in or pulled to something. The feeling was odd, and I could not fully understand it.

As I drew closer to Santiago, it became clearer to me what was happening. I felt that I was being beckoned, as if someone was waiting for me. I instinctively knew that someone was Christ.

I am not able to explain exactly what was taking place in my heart. It was both a longing for and a being called to. While I was experiencing Christ as I walked, I was increasingly being consumed by the reality that he was waiting for me in Santiago. I have never since had such a genuine sense of God waiting on me.

I expected this feeling to subside once I arrived at the cathedral, but it did not. In fact it only grew more powerful. I expected Mass to satisfy, and while it did bring clarity, there was something else.

This Is Beauty

It was not until later in the afternoon, when I found the eucharistic adoration chapel, that my insatiable thirst for God was satisfied. It was there that I met Jesus, who was waiting for me. The instant I walked into the chapel, I encountered the

One who had been drawing me to himself for the last five hundred miles.

I knelt in silence. I felt as if my chest had been torn open, and light—rich, living, healing light—flooded my very being. The One who is wholly eternal consumed the place where I too am eternal, my soul. At that moment there was a union or communion that was as real as any other personal encounter I have ever experienced.

I knelt in front of the Blessed Sacrament and was in awe of Christ's beauty. I silently prayed. After some time I found myself repeating, "This is beauty."

Over the previous month I had seen much beauty. There was the natural beauty of the mountains and plains, the prairies and fields, the streams and lakes. There was the beauty of the magnificent Gothic cathedrals and humble stone chapels. The beauty in my fellow pilgrims showed me the countless faces of God, and many of them will be stamped in my memory for all time.

But none of this compared to the beauty in front of me. Or perhaps all of the beauty was consumed in the One before whom I was kneeling. God was present. His words echoed through my very being.

"I will not leave you orphaned" (John 14:18, NRSV).

"I am with you always, to the close of the age" (Matthew 28:20).

"I have called you by name" (Isaiah 43:1).

"You did not choose me, but I chose you" (John 15:16).

"Bear the fruit that must endure" (see John 15:16).

God had called me and was calling me to himself.

Many times over the years of my life, I had heard God call my name, always inviting me to a life of grace and mercy. Sometimes the call was simply asking me to get out of bed to pray, while at other times it was that more monumental asking for all of my life as a priest. I have prayed for the grace to always say yes, to not delay and never walk away. And at that moment in a little side chapel in the cathedral of Santiago, I sensed that God was pleased with my yes, that he was delighted with my humble thank-you.

I was in awe. There were no more words, no more prayers of petition, no more questions, no more wonderings about what was to come—only presence, only love.

I knelt before Christ in utter silence, without movement, and was available to the One who was present to me.

Your Camino

God was, and is, always waiting. There is never a time when he is not longing for us to come to him. The invitation is ever-present. The human heart was made for God and will only be fully satisfied when in union with him. How correct Saint Augustine was when he said that our hearts are restless until they rest in God. If we are quiet and still, we can feel his tugging; we can detect his summons. He is always calling us to more and wanting to draw us to himself.

Our very life is a pilgrimage, always being enticed further, being brought closer to Christ. At times our lives are too chaotic for us to hear God's invitation, but if you are able to get away from the madness and be still, you can hear it; you can sense it.

It is in the quiet that we understand why we are walking. It is in the stillness that we more fully understand what or whom we are walking toward.

I don't always experience God as profoundly as I did in the chapel in Santiago, but I know that any time I make myself present to the Author of Life, this will have an effect on me. I may not fully understand at the moment how this is, but I have total faith that it is.

After I left the adoration chapel, I e-mailed my family to let them know that I had made it. I realize that walking over five hundred miles (or 1,024,853 steps, according to Father Joe's pedometer) in thirty-one days is not the most amazing feat; it was not as if I had climbed Mount Everest. But I did have a great sense of accomplishment and was excited to share it with my loved ones.

I told my family that there was nothing complicated about the Camino. All I had to do was get up each day and walk. At times it was very hard, while at other times it was a great joy. But it was never complex.

This is the case in the spiritual life, too. If you want to receive the prize prepared for you from the beginning of time, you only need to keep walking. There will be times when it will be tremendously difficult, and every part of you will cry out for you to stop. But you mustn't.

Take a moment and be still. Pray for the strength to go on, and begin walking again. The grace will be there, and you can do it. Small steps. One foot in front of the other.

There will be other times when the walk will be filled with great joy and beauty. Whatever the case, God is present.

Months after the Camino I shared this with a friend who was

having a particularly difficult time. I waxed eloquent in encouraging her to just keep on walking, slowly, step by step, and assuring her that she would eventually be OK. She was quiet for a moment and then blurted out, "Father Dave, I don't even know if I am on the right path. How can I keep walking?"

Well, I hadn't thought about that. However, in a moment of inspiration, I remembered Teresa and Anthony from Brazil. I recounted their story and stated, "Sometimes when you feel you can't go on and can't even see if you are on the right path, you need to walk with someone who is able to see and whom you trust to know the correct path. You will need to place your left hand on that person's shoulder and begin walking again."

It all seems really simple to me. What the world needs more of are pilgrims heading to the house of the Father, pilgrims who will follow in Christ's footsteps. If you know the way, then have the courage to lead someone who doesn't. If you are lost and don't know where you are going, find someone who is on the right path, and hold on till you can walk by yourself.

Pilgrim People

I recall once again what Saint Peter wrote: "For to this you have been called, because Christ also suffered for you, leaving you an example, that you should follow in his steps" (1 Peter 2:21). Following Christ is difficult, and because of this some people quit. Jesus said that the road that leads to life is narrow, and few people choose it. So why are we constantly surprised at the struggle?

This is what is needed: men and women who will choose to walk on the narrow path and who won't stop walking. We need men of integrity and honesty who will honor their wives, love their children and stand for what is good and true no matter what the cost. We need women who will love unselfishly and lay down their lives for their husbands and children. We need young people who will use their passion and zeal for the service of the gospel and the building up of the kingdom of God.

Often I find myself praying for a new outpouring of God's Holy Spirit on the Church. I pray for a revival that will stir our hearts to totally live for Christ. "Normal" Christian living just isn't going to cut it; it never has, and it never will. Lukewarm Christianity nauseates God (see Revelation 3:15-16)! Our response to Christ's call—and we each have a call—must be total, and it must be radical. We have to be willing to offer everything we are to God.

Invite him to strip you of everything so that you may follow him with reckless abandon. This does not necessarily mean that you will be called to leave your home and go live in some foreign land or walk across Spain. Rather, it means that you totally and without compromise turn over every part of your life to Christ and constantly choose to live for him.

The gospel demands that we no longer walk just for ourselves but that we move forward for the One who has given all for us. This is the only path to true happiness and the one that leads to the house of the Father. I am certain that with the help of God and his grace, nothing will be able to keep you from the life you have been created to live. To him be the glory.

In the end my student was correct. The Camino is Jesus. In moments of grace I was able to see him in each step I took. But a funny thing has happened: I still see him. I see him in places where I did not recognize him before and experience him in ways that I missed in the past. I have come to understand more fully that all of life reveals Jesus.

Of course he was always there: It is not he who changed but rather I. I continually pray that my life may be a reflection of his. I pray that I will be a holy priest, willing and able to offer my life for him and the people he has called me to serve. I pray that I will forever have on my heart and lips the desire to offer my life to him who is my King.

Pour obtenir à Saint-Jacques de Compostelle "LA COMPOSTELLA", faites tamponner à chaque étape.

DATE ET CACHET DE LA HALTE
FIRMAS Y SELLOS

DATE ET CACHET DE LA HALTE
FIRMAS Y SELLOS